# A World of Presidia
## Food, Culture & Community

Slow Food Editore

Authors
Anya Fernald, Serena Milano, Piero Sardo

Contributors
Andrea Bufka, Didier Chabrol, Paolo Di Croce, Carlo Fanti,
Maurizio Fraboni, John Irving, Maya Jani, Marjolein Kooistra, Robert La Valva,
Gabor Lövei, Gabrio Marinozzi, James Marsden, Ilaria Morra, Raffaella Ponzio,
Loreta Sardo, Gien Teo, Sara Tramontini, Hielke van der Meulen,
Hans-Jakob Werlen, Winnie Yang

Editorial Coordination
Maria Vittoria Negro

Graphic Design
Mauro Olocco

Photographs
Giovanni Bellingeri, Nelius Buckley, Rémi Denecheau, Paolo Di Croce, Czarnego Dunajaca,
Carlo Fanti, Anya Fernald, Tino Gerbaldo, Jean-Claude Le Berre,
Marcello Marengo, Serena Milano, Alberto Peroli, Loreta Sardo, Paola Vanzo,
Francisco Klimscha, Przemek Krzakiewicz

With thanks to
The coordinators and supporters of the Presidia

Cover Photo
Sateré Mawé woman collecting Guaranà
Photo by Rémi Denecheau (RDV Production)

Photo Processing
Imago - Cuneo

Printer
L'Artistica - Savigliano (CN)

Printed in October 2004 - First Edition
Printed on Acid Free paper, Cartiera Miliani Fabriano SpA

Slow Food Editore srl
Via della Mendicità Istruita, 45
12042 Bra (CN) Italy
Tel. +39 0172 419 611 fax +39 0172 411218
info@slowfood.it - www.slowfood.it

The Presidia are a project of the Slow Food Foundation for Biodiversity.
For more information about the Foundation contact:
Silvia Aimasso, Secretary of the Foundation
Tel. +39 0172 419 701
foundation@slowfood.it
www.slowfoodfoundation.com

To support the Foundation contact:
Olivia Reviglio - Andrea Bufka
Tel. +39 0172 419 606
info@slowfoodfoundation.com

ISBN 88-8499-085-8

# Table of Contents

## Ancient Cultures, New Stories

The book that you're holding can be read in different ways. You can flip through it, look at the colorful photos, and in seeing the great diversity of faces, shapes, colors, and landscapes, wonder at what a combination of human ingenuity and agricultural biodiversity can produce. Many countries shown here are ones that we know little about; we may know one person from the country or the name of their capital city, but if we had to identify five typical foods, five major crops, or a traditional beverage, we'd be hard-pressed to respond.

I recommend you read the stories told in this book and not just look at the pictures—even if you are not particularly interested in agricultural biodiversity, food, or international trade regulations. These well-documented descriptions of the 65 products tell the stories of individuals who are working with dedication to safeguard their cultures. These stories are an unconventional take on the themes of globalization and the environment. Without a single overarching statement to make, without tables, and with few statistics, this book tells the stories of farmers, cultures, and products. With this approach, we want to tell you about an alternative to industrial agriculture. An alternative we describe as a style of life, a style of working with the earth, one that respects the environment, and creates good-tasting foods that deserve to be seen outside the context of restrictive import and hygeine laws and customs controls. These food producers deserve to earn a decent living and to be able to escape their increasing marginalization in today's global market. In these pages, we may touch on themes that you hear little about in the mainstream media: the daily work of farmers; people cooking and preparing food with ancient techniques; people who are trying to adapt their agricultural techniques to climate change; the impoverishment of biodiversity; and the disappearance of animal breeds and local fruits and vegetables. We are using the words of the farmers themselves to tell these stories, and you'll see some similarities among the struggles that are being faced by farmers in different countries, notwithstanding the differences among their cultures and products.

All these projects are the scope and objective of the Slow Food Foundation for Biodiversity. The Foundation works to sustain, promote, and raise the profile of these artisan foods through the Presidia recounted in this book, among other projects. A part of the cover price of this book goes directly to the Foundation, and we ask that those who believe in and support these projects help us in our work. This is the new challenge for the Slow Food movement, which will succeed only with the help of our members, friends, and supporters.

Piero Sardo
*President, Slow Food Foundation for Biodiversity*

# A World
# of Presidia

Slow Food's Presidia began in Italy in 1999 as a development of the Ark of Taste project, which had cataloged hundreds of products at risk of disappearance. While Ark of Taste is a descriptive list of exceptional products in danger of disappearing, Presidia are local projects that focus on a group of producers of a single product and develop production and marketing techniques to allow them to be economically viable. The Presidia projects work to promote sustainable land management, cooperation among producers, and recognition of the wisdom of food artisans. 'Presidia' in Latin means 'garrison' or 'fort', and the Presidia are just that: a safe haven for great foods that protects them against the tide of globalized food production. The first Presidia project—to save the Morozzo Capon — was in the region of Piedmont, where the international Slow Food movement is based. The second, in Tuscany — another center of Slow Food activity — was the Zolfino Bean Presidium. Initially, it was difficult to explain the project model to Piedmontese and Tuscan farmers, and Slow Food's efforts were met with some suspicion. But doubts faded as the project proved a success, and at Salone del Gusto in 2000, the section of the event dedicated to the first 90 Italian Presidia attracted incredible interest. The Presidia were mobbed with people curious to see and taste rare cheeses, unusual cured meats, and heirloom fruit and vegetable varieties. Producers were eager to create Presidia for they increased

## 65 Projects in 30 Countries

sales; a study by Milan's Bocconi University in 2002 showed an average increase in sales of 42% in the first year of Presidia development. After 2000, the Presidia projects started to grow around the world with the first International Presidia.

While the Italian Presidia are always for a single product with historic ties to one area and clearly defined production techniques, some of the International Presidia were developed along new lines that conserved the same spirit and philosophy. For example, in the United States, a new Presidium model was created to promote artisan makers of raw milk cheese. This Presidium unites a group of producers around a political food issue rather than an existing product (page 84). For other Presidia, the taste quality of the product—always an important factor—had to be evaluated differently to take into account different food cultures, history and knowledge. In Presidia in the developing world, the project often takes into consideration socio-cultural and environmental aspects. For example, the Presidia project might promote the involvement of women or schooling for the producers' children in environmental practices. In this part of the world the Presidia are not only about preserving a gastronomic tradition, but may also aid in developing a product through providing technical advisors like an agronomist, organizing work experiences, or buying equipment such as a huller, harvester, or a vacuum-packer.

In the past two years the number of Presidia has more than tripled. Ideas, strategies, and themes have matured, and these developments have been shared at the Salone del Gusto 2004 and in many Earth Workshops and meetings at Terra Madre, Slow Food's World Meeting of Food Communities, held in Turin, Italy, in October 2004. For instance, the Red Fife Wheat Presidium (Canada, page 54) has become one of the symbols of the battle for GM-free agriculture, while Dehradun Basmati Rice (India, page 98), Bario Rice (Malaysia, page 102) and Andasibe Red Rice (Madagascar, page 18) celebrate the extraordinary biodiversity of rice, the world's most important food. A number of Latin American Presidia work to defend forest resources and promote agroforestry as a sustainable farming technique, such as the Pando Brazil Nut (Bolivia, page 38), Saterè Mawè Guaranà (Brazil, page 48), and Chinantla Vanilla (Mexico, page 74). The battle for the defense of raw milk is fought most importantly with Presidia in those countries that suffer the most from draconian hygiene standards in milk and artisan production: the United States (page 84) and Ireland (page 136). The issue of safeguarding native breeds and the quality of meat with attention to animal well-being and feed is addressed through projects for meat and cured meats such as the Rennes Coucou Chicken (France, page 118), Reindeer Suovas (Sweden, page 164), Euskal Txerria Pig (Spain, page 154), Mangalica Sausage

(Hungary, page 132), and many others.

In addition to the battle for raw milk production, the cheese Presidia promote the defense of mountain agriculture: from Oscypek produced in the Tatra mountains Poland, (page 146) to cheese made from yak milk on plains above 4,500 meters in altitude in ethnic Tibet (China, page 94). The appreciation of agriculture of highlands and marginal regions is also the central theme of the Peruvian Presidia, the Andean Potatoes (page 82) and Andean Fruit (page 80) cultivated on stone terraces at up to 3,900 meters. Another theme is the defense of origins, especially of those products that we are accustomed to buying mixed or in extract form without any knowledge of their provenance or producers such as coffee, cacao and vanilla. Many new countries have become part of the International Presidia in the past two years: Canada, Sweden, Chile, Ecuador, Madagascar, São Tomé and Princípe, Hungary, Bosnia-Herzegovina, China, and Croatia. In France, the past year has seen the development of five projects, and Brazil's four new Presidia have garnered the support of the Ministry of Agricultural Development, thanks to an important accord signed in 2004 by Carlo Petrini and the Brazilian Minister of Agriculture. In 2004 the Presidia initiated exchanges between projects in different countries. Through the support of the Region of Tuscany and their research agency ARSIA, in May 2004, Polish butchers and breeders of the Oscypek Presidium came to Italy to visit the Zeri Lamb Presidium, Alpago Lamb Presidium and the Pecorino of Pistoia Mountain Sheep Cheese Presidium. In June, fishermen from Robinson Crusoe Island in Chile and those of the Narta Lagoon in Albania met the Orbetello fishermen's cooperative to learn about efficient forms of sustainable aquaculture. The exchanges will continue in the next few years; one in particular will bring producers of prosciutto and cured meat from various Presidia to the Spanish Real Iberico Consortium to learn refined production techniques and learn about free-range pig ranching from the Consortium's system of animal husbandry, in which black pigs forage in the dehesa, a primordial oak forest that covers whole regions of northwest Spain.

This is only the beginning. The Chamber of Commerce of Turin, which promotes the development of exchanges with businesses around the world, is interested in supporting collaboration between Presidia producers and a group of outstanding artisan producers—among the best in the world—from the Province of Turin. The opportunity to collaborate with these Piedmontese artisans will help communities from less developed countries, and it will also help the producers from Turin learn more about raw materials (coffee, cacao, vanilla, rice) from those who produce it and to explore the difficulties linked to the global market.

# How are Presidia Created?

There is no single procedure that specifies how to start a Presidium, as the approach varies based on the type of product and the specific cultural and gastronomic characteristics of the region of production. Normally the process begins with the identification of an interesting product.

A Presidium nomination can come from a Slow Food Convivium leader, a Slow Food member, a journalist or technician, a chef, or a member of the Jury for the Slow Food Award for the Defense of Biodiversity, or from the producers themselves.

At this point, Slow Food researches the historic nature of the product, its production area, cultivation techniques (or breeding or processing), its producers, and so on. Then, the product is tasted. Gastronomic excellence is foremost amongst the criteria for selection of the International Ark Commission; although the concept of quality is relative to various social and cultural contexts, the basic idea of taste pleasure is the same whether in Italy or Guatemala.

Aspects such as links to the territory, artisanality and the size and sustainability of producer organizations are evaluated, and if the product meets the necessary requirements, it is then ready to join the Ark of Taste—Slow Food's catalog of products at risk of extinction—but that does not automatically mean that the product will become a Presidium.

To form a Presidium, two other elements are fundamental: the presence of a local coordinator who can follow the development of the project on a volunteer basis, and the availability of a producer group to work to address the technical issues of production and establish a production protocol.

Very often the person who nominates a Presidium becomes the coordinator, unaware of the great responsibility that the Presidium work will bring in the years to follow! Managing a project of this kind means confronting many difficulties but also learning about territory, food culture, and the local market from top to bottom.

The availability of the producers is also essential, as all of the work of the Presidium builds upon their collaboration. Collaboration between the original members of the group of producers must be followed also by their openness to recruit new Presidium producers in the future. The number of producers is never 'closed'—as one goal of the Presidia project is to increase the number of artisan food producers that are rigorous and attentive to taste and sustainability.

The two primary conditions—availability and interest of producers, and the presence of a local coordinator—must be verified on site by visiting the areas of production, meeting local partners (Slow Food Convivium leaders, technicians, and institutions) and conducting a preliminary meeting with producers.

## What Does a Presidium Do?

The development of each Presidium has a number of key steps.

First of all, the Presidium brings together the producers, technicians, experts, and institutions that are relevant to the project.

Then the Presidium identifies the production area and, through meetings with individual producers, collects the information necessary to establish a Production Protocol, an important instrument for guaranteeing traceability, artisanality and excellent product quality.

Next, the Presidium helps the producers to form an association (or cooperative, consortium, etc.) with a name and brand. In developing countries, technical assistance may be necessary, as well as small investments in infrastructure (for example, a rice huller).

Finally, the Presidium communicates: it tells consumers all around the world about this extraordinary product and that seeking it out, buying it and tasting it is well worth the effort. Slow Food's communication presents Presidia foods as a way to understand the history and traditions of a place and to preserve gastronomic culture. Much of the communication about the Presidia is promoted through Slow Food's guides, magazines, events, and books like the one you're holding.

## The Foundation: How the Presidia are Funded

Presidia projects have a number of costs. On-site costs include visits, producers' meetings, and the development of an association. Promotional costs include the development and publication of communications materials such as articles, brochures and posters, and participation in Slow Food's major events. Presidia in the developing world have additional costs associated with technical assistance and small investments in infrastructure. However, the Presidia do not have direct income, as the producers do not pay to become part of the project, nor does Slow Food earn from the sale of their products. In some cases in developed countries, the producers' association themselves may be able to contribute directly to the overhead costs (stands at events, brochures, translations), although this is the exception, not the rule. To help bridge the gap, Slow Food created the Slow Food Foundation for Biodiversity in 2003 with the support of the Region of Tuscany in order to gather financial resources and distribute them transparently. The Foundation is the economic support behind all Slow Food's international efforts to preserve agricultural biodiversity: The Presidia, the Ark of Taste and the Slow Food Award for the Defense of Biodiversity. Supporters of the Foundation can be public bodies, institutions, private companies or individuals. The Foundation can be supported through its general fund or also by the 'adoption' of a specific project. The role of the International Slow

Food movement is fundamental to the success of the Presidia project; around the world the Convivia organize events and collect funds to support the Presidia (opportunities for exchange between countries often emerge from these initiatives) and five Euro of every annual membership fee goes to the Foundation. Furthermore, part of the revenue from each major international event organized by Slow Food is dedicated to the Foundation. Even the Italian Presidia support the Presidia in the developing world. Since 2003, a portion of the funds raised to support each Presidium in Italy is set aside for the benefit of the International Presidia. In Italy there are also a number of significant sponsors that support the Presidia on a national level: the Ministry of Agriculture and Forestry, Coop Italia and Berlucchi. Finally, those whose donations to the Foundation take the form of technical expertise and hard work must be acknowledged: veterinarians, artisans, cheesemakers, pastry chefs, and many more. They are cited in each Presidium description as the project's 'Technical Partner'.

## Chronology: Slow Food's Projects for Agricultural Biodiversity

*Slow Food was historically a movement of gourmets—food consumers— dedicated to the promotion of the pleasures of the table and of fine wine. A decade ago, the movement began to develop in a new direction, reaching out to food producers and working with them to protect traditional products. This timeline recounts some of the key steps in that transition.*

**1996** - Ark of Taste founded at the first Salone del Gusto in Turin.

**1997** - Ark of Taste Manifesto defined the Ark's objectives: to document and safeguard an extraordinary economic, social and cultural heritage of local gastronomy.

**1999** - Scientific Ark Commission, made up of Slow Food experts, journalists, professors and researchers, defined methods and criteria for research.

**2000** -The first Presidia, projects that protect Ark products, are created. At the national level, Italian companies such as Guido Berlucchi and Coop Italia support the Presidia, while on the local level agricultural institutions, development agencies, and businesses become involved.

**2001** - The first International Presidium created in India to save artisan production of Mustard Seed Oil.

**2002** - The first twenty International Presidia are presented at the Salone del Gusto and the International Ark Commission is founded to identify general criteria and develop the Ark around the world.

**2003** - The Slow Food Foundation for Biodiversity is formed to fund all of Slow Food's activities in defense of agricultural biodiversity: the Presidia, the Ark of Taste and the Slow Food Award for the Defense of Biodiversity.

**2004** - 65 International Presidia from 30 countries gather in Turin, Italy for the Salone del Gusto 2004 and to participate in Terra Madre, World Meeting of Food Communities.

# Supporters of the Slow Food Foundation for Biodiversity

**Founding Partner**
Region of Tuscany

**Honorary Members**
Region of Tuscany
Coop Italia

**Benefactors**
(Specific Presidia Adopters)

**Beppino Occelli**
Polish Red Cow (Poland)

**Castello di Verduno**
Gamonedo (Spain)

**Consorzio Tutela Vino Lessini Durello**
Niotiko (Greece)

**Consorzio Tutela Vini Oltrepò Pavese**
Anishinaabeg Manoomin (USA)

**Eurochocolate**
Nacional Cacao (Ecuador) and Monkó Cacao (Saõ Tomé and Príncipe)

**La Montecchia**
Mirandesa Sausage (Portugal)

**Planeta**
Dehradun Basmati Rice (India)

**Province of Arezzo**
Mustard Seed Oil (India) and Jamao Coffee (Dominican Republic)

**Region of Piedmont**
Andean Corn and Yacón (Argentina)

**Region of Sicily-Regional Ministry of Agriculture and Forestry**
Chinantla Vanilla (Mexico)

**Region of Veneto**
Presidia in Brazil

**Saclà**
Andean Potatoes (Peru)

**Sámiid Riikasearvi (Sámi Association of Sweden)**
Reindeer Suovas (Sweden)

**Seven municipalities and the Po Delta Regional Park (Emilia-Romagna)**
Andasibe Red Rice and Mananara Vanilla (Madagascar)

**Slow Food Scandicci Convivium**
Mangalica Sausage (Hungary)

**Trace Foundation**
Tibetan Plateau Yak Cheese (China)

**Trasimeno-Medio Tevere Mountain Community,
Slow Food Trasimeno Convivium and the Municipality of Corciano**
Canapu Cowpea (Brazil)

**Twenty-three Roero Winemakers**
Oscypek (Poland)

## Sustainers

Slow Food Alto Vicentino Convivium
Slow Food Oristano Convivium
Agricoltori del Chianti Geografico
Roberto Anselmi
Apabiol
Araldica
Association of Moscato Passito producers from Bagnario di Strevi Valley
Autonomous Province of Bolzano - Ministry of Finance and Development
Chamber of Commerce of Benevento
Chamber of Commerce of Bolzano
Chamber of Commerce of Roma
Camigliano
Cantina Sociale di Dolcetto di Clavesana
Castello Banfi
Cirmont - International Mountain Research Center
Municipality of Coggiola
Municipality of Conca Casale
Municipality of Delia
Municipality of Ozieri
Municipality of Saracena
Municipality of Savona
Municipality of Sinagra
Municipality of Siniscola
Mountain Community of High Tanaro Valley
Mountain Community of Cesenate Apennines
Mountain Community of Media Valle del Serchio
Mountain Community of the Florentine Mountain
Mountain Community of Monti Dauni Meridionali
Mountain Community of Reventino, Tiriolo and Mancuso
Mountain Community of Terminio Cervialto
Mountain Community of Curone Grue and Ossona Valleys
Consortium du Noir de Bigorre
Consorzio del Vino Nobile di Montepulciano
Coop Liguria
Coppo
Donnafugata
Febvre & Co
Feudi di San Gregorio
Gal Le Macine
Gruppo Italiano Vini
Les Communautés de Communes du Pays de Saint-Flour et de la Planèze
Lurisia
Lungarotti
Menodiciotto Il Gelato
Mulino Marino
Cilento and Vallo di Diano National Park
Gran Sasso and Monti della Laga National Park
Pollino National Park
Po Delta Regional Park (Emilia-Romagna)
Prealpi Giulie Regional Park
Pasqua Vigneti Cantine
Province of Arezzo
Province of Lodi
Province of Pistoia
Province of Reggio Emilia
Saiagricola-Cascina Veneria
Terre Da Vino

# Africa

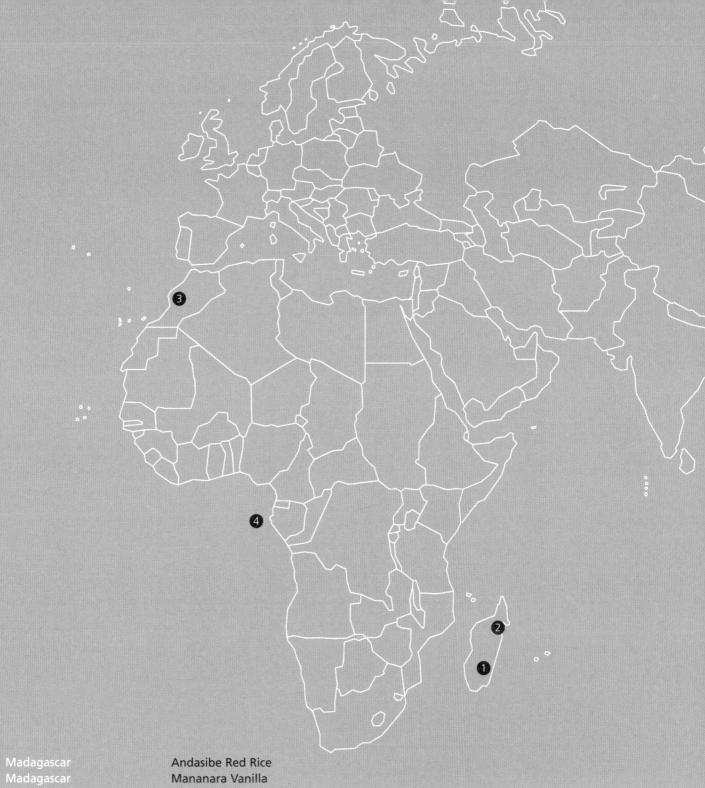

| 1 | Madagascar | Andasibe Red Rice |
| 2 | Madagascar | Mananara Vanilla |
| 3 | Morocco | Argan Oil |
| 4 | São Tomé and Príncipe | Monkó Cacao |

# Andasibe Red Rice

## Vary Mena— Native Rice

Malgasy farmers eat rice three times a day: at breakfast cooked in porridge with wild greens; at lunch with chili peppers and salt; and at dinner accompanied with stewed chicken, fried eggs, black-eyed peas, lentils, or pounded cassava leaves. With their meal they drink *ranon 'apango*: water boiled with the burned crust of rice in the cooking pot. All told, rice provides up to 70% of their daily calories; it is their mainstay, primary crop, and also weighted with deep religious and ritual significance.

In Madagascar, all varieties of locally grown rice fetch the same price at market, but there is one variety, a dusty red grain, that sells out before the others.

Called *vary mena* in local dialect, this red rice is considered Madagascar's indigenous variety. *Vary mena* may be descended from Madagascar's native rice varieties: Indonesian settlers who colonized Madagascar around 1000 most likely brought white japonica varieties with them which then mixed with the wild strains of African red rice present on the island. The result is a half-African, half-Asian variety with a rich nutty flavor. According to local folklore, the best *vary mena* is always reserved for the elderly and the infirm, as it is thought to be more nutritious than white rice.

Madagascar's 'rice bowl' produces the vast majority of the country's rice; a stretch of highland that spreads across the south-east provinces, it is increasingly a zone of conflict between small farmers and environmentalists. As Madagascar is one of the centers of the world's biological biodiversity (90% of the species found on the island are endemic), international conservation groups are working to

## The Presidium

Because of its wild heritage, Andasibe Red Rice, or *vary mena*, yields less than hybrid white varieties. It does not fetch a higher price at the local markets, and what does arrive at market in the cities is poorly processed. However, *vary mena* has been shown to have the potential for higher yields and using new agricultural techniques with this ancient variety may give new promise to commercial cultivation.

The Andasibe Red Rice Presidium combines an innovative agricultural approach (the System of Rice Intensification) with the promotion of five indigenous red rice varieties. This technique gives high yields with minimum impact on the environment and, most importantly, it is an economically viable alternative to slash-and-burn cultivation.

The Presidium is run in collaboration with the Tongalaza Kolo Harena Farmers' Federation, which represents Kolo Harena farmer associations in the cities of Ambatavola, Beforona, and Andasibe. The Presidium has invested in rice hulling and cleaning equipment, packaging, and labeling for the Kolo Harena association to enable them to have a transportable and durable product capable of competing with imported varieties on the local market.

reduce the impact of agriculture on the island's rich wildlife. The Analamazotra-Andasibe National Park, in the northern part of Madagascar's 'rice bowl', anchors the southernmost tip of the longest corridor of primary forest still intact in Madagascar, which links the Analamazotra-Andasibe, Mantadia, and Zahamena nature reserves. The farms in the Presidium project are on the edge of the Analamazotra-Andasibe reserve in the eastern part of Madagascar, part of the 'buffer zone' of sustainable agriculture in which various NGOs are working to develop around one of Madagascar's last remaining forest corridors.

| Production Area | Producers | Presidium Coordinator | Presidium supported by |
|---|---|---|---|
| Madagascar<br>Tamatave Province<br>Municipalities of Ambatavola, Beforona and Andasibe | 1425 farmers in 115 associations united in the *Kolo Harena Tongalaza* and *Hanitriniala* Cooperatives<br><br>**Technical Partner**<br>Risi & Co-Gli Aironi (Italy) | Glenn A. Lines<br>Regional Director, LDI Moramanga<br>Tel. +261 205682280<br>GAL@chemonics.mg | Seven municipalities—Bagnacavallo (RA), Borgonovo Val Tidone (PC), Brisighella (RA), Castel San Pietro Terme (BO), Castelnuovo Rangone (MO), Cavriago (RE), Fontanellato (PR)—and the Po River Regional Park, all in the region of Emilia-Romagna |

## Madagascar

# Mananara Vanilla

### In the Shade of the Forest

Vanilla was first used as a flavoring by the Aztecs and continues to grow wild today in the tropical forests of Central America; but some of the best vanilla in the world is grown far from its original homeland on the African island of Madagascar. First brought by the French colonists in 1840, vanilla found fertile soil in the humid northern rainforests of Madagascar. African vanilla soon developed a reputation for its heady scent, with strong notes of prunes, dried fruit and cloves.

Today, Madagascar produces over two-thirds of the world's vanilla, all of which is cultivated in the island's humid northern regions. Larger plantations are slowly replacing the traditional style of cultivation, in which vines are planted at the base of large trees in the rainforest.

In the UNESCO Biosphere Reserve of Mananara-Nord in the extreme northeast of the island, vanilla growers continue to use basic methods on small plots of 20 to 40 vines each. The vanilla orchids are grown in remote villages scattered around Mananara-Nord that are linked to the port only by footpaths. Mananara can be reached by car only three or four months of the year, for in the rainy season the road becomes impassable. In Mananara, vanilla blossoms are pollinated by hand using a fine stick or spine. After pollination, the flowers form seedpods that resemble fresh green beans. These are transformed by curing into dark pliable sticks with an intense, voluptuous perfume. To cure vanilla, the fresh green pods are blanched in hot water, then covered and kept in a warm location for two to three weeks. The rural producers of Mananara wrap the blanched beans in woolen blankets and store the packets on the elevated floors of their houses to keep them warm and dry. During this curing period the beans 'sweat' extra moisture and enzymes within the pods liberate vanilla's principal flavor component: vanillin. During the curing and fermentation phase, the women of Mananara rub each of the vanilla beans each day with their hands, cleaning them and rendering them supple and smooth.

## Bourbon, not Whiskey, but Vanilla

The use of the name Bourbon to describe vanilla comes from the original name for France's East-Indian colonies, which are now known as the Cormoros Islands. 'Bourbon' now is used to describe most vanilla from Madagascar, Reunion, and Mauritius, as well as that of the Cormoros Islands. The distinction was probably made initially to distinguish between the new African vanillas—originally considered of lower quality—and the traditional central American beans. The flavor of Bourbon vanillas tend to be more complex, with notes of cloves, prunes, and dried figs, and they can lack the classic clear strong vanilla note that strengthens other vanilla extracts. But in contrast to popular belief, there is no particular technique in production that makes one vanilla Bourbon and another not. The only (slight) difference in production between Bourbon and other vanillas is in the length of time in which the beans are allowed to ferment. While central American beans are often simply dried, Bourbon vanilla beans can be steamed and left to ferment for a slightly longer period of time, which may have been developed to cultivate differences in flavor, or could simply have simplòy been a step necessary to protect the vanilla from rot in the high humidity of the African islands.

## The Presidium

This Presidium is working with a group of 125 farmers in the Mananara-Nord Biosphere Reserve to improve cultivation techniques and to develop autonomy among farmers in the sale and marketing of this valuable spice. Mananara's remoteness and Biosphere Reserve status have helped conserve the traditional style of production but have also limited producers to selling only to local distributors. Although vanilla is one of the world's most precious spices, the farmers themselves receive little of the profits that this product can reap in the international market. By forming a cooperative and setting up a structure for direct purchase, the Presidium will guarantee that a higher percentage of profits are reinvested in the community.

The decision to develop this project also has a strong ecological premise: Madagascar is home to the greatest biological biodiversity in the world and the vanilla growers farm on one of the country's few national parks. By assisting the continued low-impact cultivation of vanilla instead of crops that require slash-and-burn agriculture, the Presidium is working to maintain a style of agriculture that both promotes livelihood and conserves the environment.

---

**Production Area**
Madagascar
Ten villages in the Mananara-Nord Biosphere Reserve, near the city of Mananara

**Producers**
125 farmers united in the Mpambolin' Ambanivolo Association

**Technical Partner**
Baiocco A. & Figlio (Italy)

**Presidium Coordinator**
Jürg Brand
Intercooperation
Tel. +261 20 22 60889-61205
brand@wanadoo.mg
intercop@iris.mg

**Presidium supported by**
Seven municipalities—
Bagnacavallo (RA), Borgonovo Val Tidone (PC), Brisighella (RA), Castel San Pietro Terme (BO), Castelnuovo Rangone (MO), Cavriago (RE), Fontanellato (PR)— and the Po River Regional Park, all in the region of Emilia-Romagna

# Argan Oil

## Oil from the Desert

The argan tree is native to the southern coast of Morocco between the cities of Safi and Goulimime. It is little known and grows only in a region of about 12,000 square kiloneters. Argan is well adapted to the harsh environment of the southern Moroccan coast; its thick roots spread wide and deep, drawing water from the dry soil. About 20 million of the trees remain in Morocco, and UNESCO has declared the stretch of land covered with the trees (the *Arganerie*) a Biosphere Reserve. The *Arganerie* helps maintain the balance of the region bordering the Sahara and keeps the desert at bay.

The fruit of the argan has a green, fleshy exterior like an olive, but is larger and rounder. Inside the fruit, there is a nut with a hard shell that contains one, two, or three almond-shaped kernels. Almost 50 kilos of seeds are necessary to produce just half a liter of oil. For this reason, the price of the oil is very high.

In Morocco, the production of argan oil is women's work. With simple, repetitive movements, the women break the hard shells of the pits, and extract and chop the kernel. They add a few drops of warm water to this rough paste to help extract the oil, and the mixture is pressed in the *azgr*, a small mill made from two large stones, one balanced atop the other.

Argan oil is a deep golden yellow in color and the flavor is clean-cut and intense, with notes of hazelnut and toast. A few drops added to a freshly cooked pot of couscous or to a fish or meat *tajine* gives the flavor a rounded depth. Mixed with almonds and honey, argan oil is used for *amlou beldi*, the traditional creamy spread that is offered to visitors together with bread and mint tea as a sign of welcome.

Women of the Amal Cooperative breaking Argan nuts

## The Presidium

In Tamanar, a university professor from Rabat, Zoubida Charrouf, has brought together a group of Berber women in the Amal cooperative (one of the winners of the 2001 Slow Food Award). The Amal cooperative was among the first all-female cooperatives in Morocco to produce Argan Oil. Now, the Presidium works with four such cooperatives. The women of the cooperatives husk the Argan seeds, which are then pressed with modern presses instead of with the traditional pair of stones. This new industry provides an important income for the women, who often have few opportunities for work outside the home. This Presidium supports the work of the cooperatives by seeking new outlets for the sale of Argan Oil.

**Production Area**
Morocco
Essaouira, Taroudant, and Chtouka Ait Baha Provinces

**Producers**
Eighty women united in four cooperatives (Amal, Ajddigue de Tidzi, Taitmatine and Targante), joined in the umbrella group Targanine

**Technical Partner**
Olio Roi and Organic Oils (Italy)

**Presidium Coordinators**
Zoubida Charrouf
Tel. +212 37682848
zcharrouf@menara.ma

Amina Idelcadi
Tel. +212 44788381

In June 2003, Franco Boeri, an Italian producer of olive oil (Olio Roi), and Giuseppe Matticari, owner of the seed-oil company Organic Oils, visited Morocco to share ideas with the women of the Argan Oil Presidium to help them improve the quality of their product. Together with the Presidium Coordinator Zoubida Zarrouf, they documented all phases of production of the Argan Oil—from the nut picking to pressing—and took samples for analysis in Italy. Their results included a technical analysis of the acidity, fat content, and solids of the Presidium Argan Oil, as well as a detailed analysis of the weak points in production that might be improved by integration of some new techniques.

The reforms that were proposed were not revolutionary, and Boeri and Matticari suggested nothing that significantly changed their traditional nature of production, but had ideas for small and simple improvements. For example, the women needed to store the nuts better before producing the oil and to keep them cooler to avoid rancidity, or to press them sooner to avoid deterioration.

Next, Boeri and Matticari recommended regular cleaning of the pressing machines, and covering the machines and storage barrels to protect them from contact with light. Their final suggestions described how to improve the quality of the filtration, which resulted in a net improvement of the clarity and quality of the oil. Boeri and Matticari advised that the cooperative of producers

# Oil Exchange

purchase stainless steel containers to hold the oil just after pressing and dark glass bottles for the final product.

These two technicians were able to suggest simple changes that improved the quality of the Presidium Argan Oil and allowed the women of the Targanine cooperatives to reach more consumers attentive to quality and to broaden their market.

This is just one example of the many possibilities for exchange between producers from the developed and less-developed worlds, a simple type of cooperation that costs little, builds human connections and friendship among producers, and can bring big changes in quality and distribution for artisan producers.

# Monkó Cacao

## In the Gulf of Guinea, Africa's First Cacao

The volcanic islands of São Tomé and Príncipe, 300 kilometers off the coast of Gabon, are a cultural frontier between Africa and Europe. Two of four islands in an archipelago that extends through the Gulf of Guinea, they cover 1,000 square meters in total. Príncipe is 250 kilometers north of São Tomé and about one-eighth its size.

In 1822, cacao was planted for the first time in Africa on Príncipe, initially as an ornamental plant for the home of the governor of the island (his son, José Ferreira Gomes, brought it back with him on a return trip from the Brazilian lowlands). It took thirty years for the colonists to realize that their decorative cacao's flourishing health could translate into commercial potential, and in 1852 the first African cacao plantation was launched on Príncipe. By the end of the nineteenth century, cacao plantations had replaced many of the islands' historic coffee plantations. From Príncipe, Gomes' cacao plants passed to Ghana's coast—the first to arrive on the African mainland—and the groundwork for the millions of tons of cacao produced today in Western Africa.

In the past 30 years, many of the ancient cacao trees from the original Brazilian stock have been substituted on a wide scale with high-yield, disease-resistant hybrids. These original varieties are known as Monkó, which means 'native' in the local creole.

For the past decade, Italian agronomist Claudio Corallo has led a group of farmers in reviving cultivation of cacao in Africa's oldest plantations in Príncipe, while working with his family to produce finished chocolate in a tiny workshop on São Tomé. This workshop is a rarity in cacao-growing regions like West Africa, which ship the vast majority of cacao to Europe and America for processing.

After the cacao pods are harvested and the beans extracted, the fresh Monkó beans are packed into wooden fermentation boxes lined with banana leaves. The fermented beans are roasted in Corallo's workshop and made into chocolate—rich, full-flavored bars with strong floral flavors and a sharp, jolting acidity.

## The Presidium

During the past eight years Cacao Monkó trees have been selected for flavor quality on the island of Príncipe, with a goal of reviving the original variety of cacao brought to Africa in the nineteenth century. The project's objective is to guarantee producers a better price and to enable them to distinguish their product from the more common hybrids produced on the island.

The Nova Moka cooperative, which purchases and commercializes cacao from the growers, guarantees a minimum price and reinvests earnings from cacao sales in the infrastructure of production. Through these earnings, the cooperative has already built a cacao dryer and many wooden fermentation boxes.

Future objectives of the project include the genetic profiling of Monkó Cacao (necessary for identifying trees), securing further autonomy among growers, and the strengthening of the infrastructure of cacao production in Príncipe with the addition of fermentation boxes and cacao dryers.

**Production Area**
Republic of São Tomé and Príncipe Príncipe Island, area around Terreiro Velho, Nova Estrela, Santo Cristo, and Praia Abade

**Producers**
120 families, some of whom are united in the *Cooperativa das Artes e Ofícios*

**Presidium Coordinator**
Claudio Corallo
Tel. +239 222 934-236
ccorallo@cstome.net

**Presidium supported by**
Eurochocolate

If the world's cacao growers were represented by 100 people, 70 would be African, 20 Asian and 10 Latin American, 90 would cultivate less than 5 hectares, 10 would own large plantations, and 75 would never have tasted a bar of chocolate in their lives.

80 percent of the chocolate market is controlled by six multinationals. Three—Mars, Philip Morris (owners of Kraft, Jacobs, Suchard, Côte d'Or, Milka) and Hershey—are American and the other three—Nestlé (Switzerland), Cadbury-Schweppes (UK) and Ferrero (Italy)—are European. The growers are just the first weak link in this long chain. The price of cacao may go up or down, but it makes little difference to them.

# Theobroma cacao cacao

## Cacao's Shapes and Forms

There are over three thousand varieties of edible cacao in the world. They can be grouped into three general classes: two subspecies and one hybrid.

**Criollo**, of the subspecies *Theobroma cacao cacao*, originated in Central America, probably from the area of the Isthmus of Panama. It was the first cacao variety to be cultivated in pre-Columbian Central America. This subspecies is very susceptible to disease, ripens late and has a relatively low yield and short productive life compared to the Forastero variety. Criollo's distinctive features are its exquisite flavor, its rich, intense taste and its full aroma.

**Forastero**, of the subspecies *Theobroma cacao sphaerocarpum*, is also known as *amazonico* or *amelonado*. Domesticated later than Criollo, Forastero's wild ancestors proliferated in the Amazon basin.

Forastero cacaos tend to be vigorous, robust plants that mature quickly and produce a rough chocolate. Forastero accounts for most of the world's production (over 90%) and is grown mainly in Africa and Asia.

**Trinitario** is a hybrid of the Criollo and Forastero subspecies that dates back to the late eighteenth century. After a natural disaster that destroyed virtually all the Criollo on the island of Trinidad, Forastero plants were imported and the few surviving Criollo trees began to hybridize with new ones to create the new Trinitario variety. Trinitario combines some of the aromatic properties of Criollo with the hardiness and higher productivity of Forastero. It has stronger aromas and a richer flavor than Forastero, but lacks some of the intensity of the Criollo varieties.

# Chocolate's Chronology

The classic chocolate bar as we know it today has existed for just over a century, but the consumption of cacao goes back 3,000 years.

**1000 BCE**
The use of *kakaw* spreads in the Olmec civilization.

**400 BCE - 1000 ADE**
Cacao adopted by the Mayas. Chocolate drinking vessels found in tombs dating to the beginning of this period.

**1521**
Hernán Cortés conquers the Aztec capital of Tenochtitlan. Europeans first encounter chocolate in liquid form, flavored with vanilla or chili pepper, the way the Aztecs and other Pre-Hispanic peoples before them used to prepare it.

**1585**
The first commercial shipment of cacao beans reaches Seville.

**1600**
Chocolate becomes the favorite beverage of the Spanish court. The cacao is made into tablets with sugar that can be dissolved in hot water. Spain remains Europe's center of quality chocolate production for the next 200 years.

**1657**
The first chocolate house opens in London. Within a century, English chocolate houses become the haunt of many London politicians, not to mention 'lowngers', who, in the words of one commentator for the popular *Spectator* magazine, "...shift Coffee-houses and Chocolate-houses from Hour to Hour, to get over the insupportable Labour of doing nothing" (1711).

**1660s**
First chocolate house opens in Florence. Francesco Redi writes that at the court of Tuscany, Mediterranean ingredients such as the fresh zest of limes and lemons and the genteel scent of jasmine are added to chocolate (*Bacchus in Tuscany*, 1685).

**1680**
The French begin to produce cacao on a large scale in Martinique.

**1765**
The first American chocolate factory opens in Massachusetts.

**1778**
The Dutch take cacao to Sumatra and establish their first major production center.

**1828**
Dutch chemist Conrad van Houten invents a process to extract cocoa butter from beans, thus producing the first cocoa powder.

**1847**
British company J.S. Fry and Company uses cocoa powder for the first mass-produced chocolate.

**1879**
Following centuries of vain attempts, chemist Henri Nestlé combines with Daniel Peter to invent the technique of mixing milk with cacao, thus producing the first milk chocolate. To solve the problem of incompatibility between the two substances, he uses a relatively unfatty powdered cacao and condensed milk (another of his inventions)

**1879**
Swiss chocolate manufacturer Rudolphe Lindt invents conching, the technique that transforms raw cacao liquor into smooth, fine-grained, mellow chocolate. Hence the modern chocolate bar is born!

# From Tree to Bean

Cacao is an evergreen tree that can produce up to 30 pods a year. It fruits directly from the trunk, the blossom budding right out of the cacao tree's bark. The tree produces pods throughout the year and the fruits take from four to six months to ripen. A cacao tree reaches maturity after four years and can remain productive for up to 30. Cacao trees can reach a height of eight to ten meters in the shade and four to six in the sun.

Cacao pods must be harvested without damaging the delicate stalk. Pickers use special machetes and cutlasses which they hold directly or secure to long poles. They then cut open the pods with knives or crack them with stones or lumps of wood and scoop out the beans and pulp. The cacao ferments straight after removal from the pod and, during the process, the white pulp is separated from the beans. Traditionally, the fresh beans are piled on a layer of branches topped with banana leaves and covered with still more beans. Today farmers leave the beans in wooden crates with drainage holes and cover them with banana leaves. Fermentation lasts from three to eight days, depending on the variety of cacao. It prevents germination, improves the flavor of the beans, and dries them slightly, while, chemically speaking, it turns the sweet pulp surrounding the cacao into alcohol, raising the temperature and acidity. This, in turn, sterilizes the bean and causes the breakdown of sugars and the transformation of some proteins into single amino-acids—all crucial phases in the refinement of the aroma of the cacao. Finally, the beans are dried.

# Americas

| 1  | Argentina      | Andean Corn                            |
| 2  | Argentina      | Yacón                                  |
| 3  | Argentina      | Quebrada de Humahuaca Andean Potatoes  |
| 4  | Bolivia        | Pando Brazil Nut                       |
| 5  | Bolivia        | Potosí Llama                           |
| 6  | Brazil         | Canapu Cowpea                          |
| 7  | Brazil         | Juçara Palm Heart                      |
| 8  | Brazil         | Sateré Mawé Native Guaranà             |
| 9  | Brazil         | Umbu                                   |
| 10 | Canada         | Red Fife Wheat                         |
| 11 | Chile          | Blue Egg Chicken                       |
| 12 | Chile          | Calbuco Black-Bordered Oyster          |
| 13 | Chile          | Merken                                 |
| 14 | Chile          | Purén White Strawberries               |
| 15 | Chile          | Robinson Crusoe Island Seafood         |
| 16 | Ecuador        | Nacional Cacao                         |
| 17 | Guatemala      | Huehuetenango Coffee                   |
| 18 | Mexico         | Chinantla Vanilla                      |
| 19 | Mexico         | Criollo Corn                           |
| 20 | Mexico         | Tehuacán Amaranth                      |
| 21 | Peru           | Andean Fruit                           |
| 22 | Peru           | Andean Potatoes                        |
| 23 | United States  | Anishinaabeg Manoomin                  |
| 24 | United States  | Cape May Salt Oyster                   |
| 25 | United States  | Heritage Turkey Breeds                 |
| 26 | United States  | Raw Milk Cheese                        |

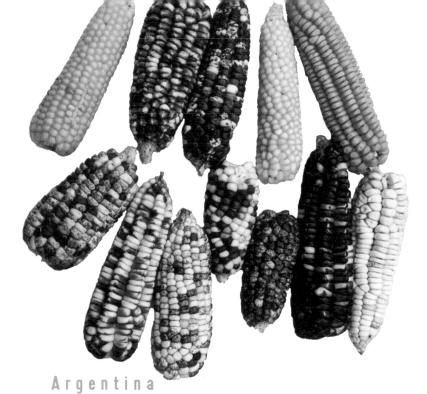

Argentina

# Andean Corn

Corn originated in the center of South America thousands of years ago; today it is one of the most widely consumed grains in the world. In northern Argentina, particularly in the province of Catamarca, many ancient varieties still exist, including Capia (reddish or white rounded kernels), Blanco Criollo (large round kernels), Amarillo Socorro (large yellow kernels, sometimes with white striations), Morocho (rounded kernels), Amarillo de Ocho (large round yellow kernels), and Chullpi (wide flat kernels).

These native corn varieties are raised in small plots, primarily for family consumption. Andean Corn farmers use ancient tools like the mule-pulled *arados de palos* plow and traditional cultivation methods. In the Catamarca province, corn is usually grown alongside peppers, potatoes, and aromatic herbs. The fields are sown by hand during the first days of October and the corn is ready to harvest in April. Before it is ready to eat, the corn must be dried completely, after which the kernels are cut off the cob and peeled. This is a lengthy, arduous process when done by hand, and the Presidium has invested in equipment for the farmers to facilitate the work of kernelling. Because the Capia variety has tender grains that shred easily, the cobs are first baked in water and lime, then peeled and dried in the sun.

Corn, along with potatoes, provides the foundation of the local population's diet. Andean culinary traditions have played an important part in safeguarding the biodiversity of these crops. Each variety has a role in the local cuisine and festivities, and cooks prepare a great variety of dishes with just a few

## The Presidium

The abandonment of rural areas, the lack of ready access to water, and the appeal of hybrid varieties have put Andean Corn varieties in real danger, and this Presidium is working to counteract these trends.

The Presidium was set up thanks to the work of agricultural researcher Juan Antonio Caseres, who has studied and cataloged Andean Corn varieties for forty years with the assistance of the Department of Agronomy at the University of Buenos Aires. The three varieties that are the focus of the Presidium's work—Amarillo Socorro, Capia, and Blanco Criollo—were chosen for their taste and agricultural qualities.

Coordinated by Slow Food convivium leader Hugo Cetrángolo and Caseres, the Presidium has obtained extraordinary results in just a few years: there is now an Association of Andean Argentinean Corn Producers that has improved quality standards and the production chain with the introduction of husking machines and a new system of preparing the corn. With the help of agronomist and chef Mayu Bacigalupo, the Association has recovered traditional corn recipes. Through the efforts of the Northern Buenos Aires Slow Food convivium, the Presidium products are being promoted for use in local restaurants.

primary ingredients. Capia corn is used to prepare *tortillas*, *tijtinchas* (a rich dish prepared for the feast of San Santiago on July 25), and *capias* (a dessert made with flour, sugar, eggs, cinnamon, and lard). Amarillo corn is used to make the famous *chicha de maiz*, an alcoholic beverage of infinite varieties drunk during special occasions, such as Carnival, and Blanco Criollo is used in *mazamorra*, a dessert that dates back to colonial times.

| Production Area | Producers | Presidium Coordinator | Presidium supported by |
|---|---|---|---|
| Argentina<br>Catamarca Province<br>Santa Maria and San José<br>Departments | 15 farming families united in the *Asociación de Productores de Maíces Andinos Argentinos* | Hugo Cetrángolo<br>Agriculture Department<br>University of Buenos Aires<br>Tel. +54 11 47712944<br>hcetrangolo@yahoo.com | Region of Piedmont |

# Quebrada de Humahuaca
# Andean Potatoes

## Four Millenia of Potato Farming

Situated at the center of Jujuy province, the Quebrada de Humahuaca is near the northern border of Argentina. The Rio Grande cuts across this dry, vividly colored landscape at altitudes varying from 2,000-4,000 meters above sea level. The great wealth of ecosystems in this region has favored the development of hundreds of edible plant species, which have been conserved and refined through the patient work of local farmers. In addition to the many varieties of potato and corn, varieties of *kiwicha*, *quinoa*, *oca* and *papa lisa*, native plants that date back to the time of the *conquistadores*, are commonly cultivated. These plants were often banned after the Europeans arrived because they were considered sacred and therefore seen as perilous sources of superstition and idolatry.

The Andean food culture is an incredible resource, both for its genetic heritage and for its economic potential. The first signs of the selection of potatoes in the Quebrada de Humahuaca date back 4,000 years, to a time when every generation maintained the tradition of cultivating a particular type of potato and often families gave their own name to the varieties they had developed and farmed.

Some communities grew a huge range of varieties of potatoes, while others specialized in seed conservation. In any case seed varieties multiplied from generation to generation and were refined through centuries of cultivation. A great part of the potato varieties once cultivated here was lost: the 70 varieties registered here 40

### The Presidium

Founded in 1996, the Cauqueva Cooperative brings together 126 small producers of potatoes, *oca*, *papa lisa* and corn. The primary objectives of the Cauqueva cooperative are to improve the quality of life for inhabitants of the Quebrada de Humahuaca through the commercialization of its traditional agricultural products, technical and agricultural assistance for farmers, and farmer education. In 2002, Cauqueva was chosen as a winner of the Slow Food Award for Biodiversity and the Presidium was founded at the beginning of 2004 to recognize the cooperative's exceptional work.

In the first year of activity, all 12 Presidium producers will receive the seeds necessary to dedicate a quarter-hectare of their land to the chosen potato varieties and will receive technical assistance in the preparation of their land for seed planting and harvesting. This assistance will be provided by the cooperative's agronomists as well as by collaborating institutions such as the Agricultural Science Faculty of Jujuy University, which will hold courses in farming, quality, variety selection, and commercialization. The Presidium will promote fresh and packaged Andean Potatoes in restaurants and on the national market. The packaged potatoes are blanched and vacuum-packed and, unlike the fresh potatoes, can be exported and sold internationally.

years ago have been reduced by more than half.

The varieties of Andean Potatoes that have survived are distinguished by their flavor, color, and high protein content. Three quarter of these varieties are part of the *Solanum tuberosum andigena* species, though there is still a good deal of debate about whether this is, in fact, a sub-species.

The Presidium has identified five varieties that are farmed at an altitude ranging from 2,100 to 3,800 meters: the Papa Azul is the sweetest potato in the group and is cylindrical with dark blue skin flecked with white and yellow flesh; the Papa Señorita, which is irregularly shaped, has white skin streaked with pink and yellowish flesh; the Cuarentilla, pink skin and white flesh; the Tuni Morada is round and flat, dark skinned with white flesh, perfect for mashing; the Chacarera, with blunted ends, white skin and white flesh, is perfect for frying. This final variety has the added curiosity that it develops violet streaks in its flesh if farmed at over 3,000 meters altitude.

| Production Area | Producers | Presidium Coordinator |
| --- | --- | --- |
| Argentina<br>Quebrada de Humahuaca<br>Jujuy Province<br>Municipalities of Tumbaya, Tilcara and Humahuaca | 12 farmers united in the Cooperativa Cauqueva (*Cooperativa Agropecuaria y Artesanal Unión Quebrada y Valles*) | Javier Rodríguez<br>Tel. +54 3884955097<br>jrcau@imagine.com.ar |

# Yacón

**The Sweetest Root in the Andes**

The origin of this ancient Andean melon-flavored root is lost in Argentina's pre-Hispanic past. In *Aimarà*, the region's indigenous language, the root is known as *aricoma* or *aricuma*, while in Spanish it is called Yacón (pronounced sha-kohn), *arboloco*, *chicama*, or *jiquimilla*. The plant is cultivated using ancient techniques and tools like the *taclla*, a wooden tool that can be traced back to the Incas. The *taclla* is used to prepare the land for planting and is then used to place the bulbs in the furrows.

Yacón is cultivated in rotation with corn or potatoes and is best harvested from August to September. This shrub has a thin trunk and green leaves and can grow to one-and-a-half meters in height. The edible part of the plant grows below ground, where the root, after being divested of its dark brown skin, boasts sweet and succulent pale yellow flesh similar in texture to a pear's. If handled gently and stored in a cool, dark place, Yacón will remain fresh for months. With time, the root sweetens further as the starches transform into sugars (a process that is accelerated by exposure to light). Once the root has been left out in the sun long enough for the skin to shrivel up, the flesh can be enjoyed raw. The people of the Quebradas also use Yacón to make juices, jams, and fruit jellies. The plant's flowers and leaves can also be used to feed cows and pigs.

The cultivation of Yacón requires a great deal of water and well-fertilized earth, and it grows well in the southern Argentine area of Quebrada de Humahuaca. The towns most noted for the production of Yacón are Barcena and Volcan, the latter an important center of production that also serves as the primary market for farmers to sell their wares. In Volcan, farmers offer their baskets of Yacón to train passengers traveling south, mostly workers from the sugarcane fields. Today, the vast majority of Yacón is consumed locally.

## The Presidium

Yacón has a great potential for development because of its superb flavor, versatility, and potential use for those who suffer from diabetes.

Slow Food will work to assist the producers of Yacón to promote their product and to find new markets in cooperation with the local association Fundandes (Foundation for the Environmental Development of Local Products).

The 30 farmers from Quebrada involved in this Presidium cultivate land that was previously abandoned or neglected or that has been converted to cultivating other crops. They continue to prepare Yacón according to traditional recipes for marmalade and savory *escabece* tea made from the plant's dried leaves.

The Presidium is working in cooperation with the Barcena Town Council to establish the production protocol for Yacón, to create an association of producers, and to promote typical products made from Yacón locally and internationally.

| Production Area | Producers | Presidium Coordinator | Presidium supported by |
|---|---|---|---|
| Argentina<br>Quebrada de Humahuaca<br>San Salvador de Jujuy | 35 families | Magda Alejandra Choque Vilca<br>Fundandes<br>Tel. +54 388 4257538<br>magui@imagine.com.ar | Region of Piedmont |

# Pando Brazil Nut

## At the Heart of the Primary Forest

The indigenous tribes of the Pando Altopiano, a Bolivian region bordering Brazil, depend on harvesting Brazil nuts for their livelihood. The kidney-shaped nuts they harvest, ivory inside and covered with reddish-brown skin, have woody shells and are enclosed in a coconut-like fruit, or coccus. The Brazil nut tree, *Bertholletia excelsa*, is a magnificent native species of the Amazon forest that reaches 40 meters in height and its thick canopy shields forest understory from the sun and rain.

It can only grow in the primary forest, where an indigenous species of bee has evolved to pass through successive layers of foliage to pollinate the flowers on the highest branches. The nuts ripen during the months of November to February, and can be gathered once they fall from the tree. Native families enter the forest carrying handmade hooked sticks, which they use to pick up the nuts from the ground so as to avoid hidden snakes. The men have the job of opening the husks containing the Pando Brazil Nuts with a few well-directed blows of a machete. After opening the coccus, they tip the nuts into the large hand-woven baskets carried on each gatherer's back (each coccus yields 15 to 20). Processing, which is mainly done by hand, involves: a homemade drier where nuts dry for about two weeks. After they are shelled with a mechanical nutcracker, the locals separate and package them according to size. Brazil nuts are eaten raw, but are also used as a base for traditional nut bars and *brigadeiros*, nuts covered in cocoa and sugar, or covered in *cupuaçu*, the sweet flesh of another fruit from the Amazon rainforest. All of these products are consumed exclusively on the local market.

## An Italian *Pasticcere* in Bolivia

In January 2004, Federico Molinari, a young Italian *pasticcere*, or pastry chef, traveled to Pando, Bolivia, to meet the Brazil nut gatherers of this region. Molinari, who owns the *Laboratorio di Resistenza Dolciaria* (Workshop of the Sweetmakers' Resistance), in the Piedmontese town of Alba, spent his time in South America helping the local women prepare traditional sweets.

In the town of Porvenir, the last outpost before the forest in Pando, the group set up a workshop with a four-burner stove, electric nut cracker, and a chopping machine. The only other equipment was an oven thermometer, a digital thermometer, two plastic spatulas, some silverware, and a few other utensils. For four days, Molinari taught these women the secrets of his trade, encouraging them to use the local materials they had on hand.

The group discussed the ways in which local ingredients could be used to best advantage, using bananas to make pastry cream and altering the traditional recipe for Bolivian *brigadeiros* (Brazil nuts covered in cacao paste and sugar) to include caramelized sugar to improve the sweets' flavor.

Next, two women from Pando are working at Molinari's workshop for two months to perfect some of their new techniques.

## The Presidium

About 60% of Pando's population have always lived from gathering nuts, but deforestation by landowners to increase land for pasture and cattle farming is cutting into the primary forest. Since the survival of the people of Pando depends on the survival of the forest, the Presidium will be setting up a project to safeguard and promote the Pando Brazil Nut. The work in Pando began with a nomination for a Presidium for this project from the NGO ACRA. With ACRA, Slow Food is now working to build a workshop where local women can produce sweets based on Pando Brazil Nuts. The first phase of the project will include the eduation of a group of producers, including two women from Pando who have come to Italy to learn from an Italian *pasticcere*. In Pando, assistance will be provided locally to ensure the post-harvesting stages (drying, packing and transport) do not compromise the quality of the product.

**Production Area**
Bolivia
Pando Department
Amazonian Region

**Producers**
14 communities in Pando with a total of 150 families of gatherers united in the COINACAPA cooperative

**Technical Partner**
Laboratorio di Resistenza Dolciaria (Italy)

**Presidium Coordinator**
Vanessa Gallo
Acra-Acei Milan
Tel. +39 02 27000291
vanessagallo@acra.it

Casildo Quispe Nina
(President, COINACAPA Cooperative)
Tel. +591 3 8422698
coinacapa@cotas.net

# Potosí
# Llama

## Rustic and Resistant

The Incas were the first to domesticate the llama, they developed an economy based almost entirely on its meat, wool, and leather. Today, llama farms are spread throughout the Andes, especially in the Potosì region of Bolivia. The pastures of Potosí range between 3,700 and 4,500 meters in altitude. The consumption of llama meat dates back at least 6,000 years, though the tradition of llama consumption was almost abandoned after the Spanish conquest. When the Spaniards introduced sheep, cows, and horses to the region, most Bolivians abandoned their llama herds and the tradition of llama husbandry lived on only among the most remote Andean tribes.

Llamas are raised at pasture and their meat is rich in protein with low fat and cholesterol. It can be eaten fresh or dried as *charque*. The technique for preparing *charque* has remained unchanged for centuries. During the winter (between May and August), the meat is thinly sliced, salted, and dried—either in the sun or in the dry cold air. The preparation of *charque* requires very little equipment: a table, a knife, and a box to hold the meat while it dries. The Andean families know how to prepare *charque* with two different techniques, either salting the slices with dry salt or using a brine bath. *Charque* is flavorful, spicy and can be conserved for long periods.

Two llama breeds have been selected and developed in the Andean highlands: the Thampulli, selected for meat production, and the K'ara, which is best for wool. Until fifty years ago, llama wool was very important for the artisan production of coats and sweaters for the local population. However, insofar as it is considered inferior to sheep wool, llama wool has been increasingly marginalized. This is due to the fact that the favored method of clipping and working the wool does not favor the production of a high quality product. However, with some simple improvements in these two phases of the production cycle, llama wool could greatly improve in quality and potentially reach a wider market. Currently, in the region of Potosí, 800,000 llama are farmed, of which 458,000 are raised in the five Potosí provinces where this project is active: Daniel Campos, Antonio Quijarro, Nor Lipez, Enrique Baldivieso and Sur Lipez.

## The Presidium

Since 1997, the NGO ACRA (Association for rural cooperation in Africa and Latin America) has worked in the Potosí region of Bolivia to sustain the work of cameloid herders. In Potosí, the llama remains popular for its meat, wool, and leather. However, to create a wider market for llama products, it is necessary to introduce methods of animal husbandry, veterinary care, animal shelter systems, and to teach new techniques for preparing wool and meat.

Potosí is a poor region that it is confronting a range of ecological and social problems. The llama industry is threatened by the erosion of pastures, blocks on exportation of llama meat, the competition from imported meat, and poor climactic conditions. In 2002, for example, a snowstorm in Sur Lipez caused the death of thousands of llamas to hunger and cold. Slow Food is sponsoring the work of ACRA to promote llama products—particularly dried *charque*. This Presidium will work to safeguard the millennial tradition of llama husbandry and thus protect an important part of Bolivia's culinary heritage.

**Production Area**
Bolivia
Potosí Region
Provinces of Daniel Campos, Antonio Quijarro, Nor Lipez, Enrique Baldivieso, and Sur Lipez

**Producers**
1101 families that are united in ARCCA (Regional Association of Cameloid Herders)

**Presidium Coordinators**
Vanessa Gallo
Acra-Acei Milan
Tel. +39 02 27000291
vanessagallo@acra.it

Japhet Zapana
Acra La Paz
Tel. +591 22421277
japhet63@hotmail.com

# Canapu Cowpea

### Black-Eyed Peas from Piauí

African slaves in the sixteenth century first brought the cowpea (*Vigna unguiculata*) to Brazil from western Africa. It became a common plant in the northeast of Brazil, and today it is generally referred to as *feijão de corda* or *feijão caupi*. This area remains a center of cowpea biodiversity and the Brazilian agricultural research agency Embrapa has selected 300 varieties. Among these is the Canapu Cowpea, which is grown in a semi-arid region in the south of Piauí.

As large as a grain of corn, the Canapu has irregular oval shapes. Like most cowpeas, the Canapu has an 'eye', a dark point, against a background color of clear green, pale pink, or bronzy yellow.

When it is cooked, the Canapu becomes dark brown with violet markings and is noted for its smoothness, flavor, and notes of freshly mown grass, hay, and walnuts.

Canapu is cultivated entirely by hand, from planting to harvest, and no chemical fertilizers or treatment is used. In the same fields where Canapu is grown, farmers plant cassava, corn, rice and cashew trees. The cashews grow alongside the cowpeas, but as their canopy grows, they crowd out shade and after four years the Canapu is no longer planted.

The Canapu Cowpea can be eaten fresh or dried, and it is an ingredient in a range of local dishes, including *mugunzá*, a dish made from corn, pork, and beans that is eaten on feast days.

Local recipes highlight the Canapu's flavor and special consistency. Locals explain that they have refused to substitute this local variety with more productive cowpea strains because of its excellent taste. The most commonly cultivated cowpea in the state of Piauí, the Canapu's market is almost exclusively local as farmers sell primarily at fairs and markets.

### The Presidium

Canapu Cowpeas are particularly interesting for their excellent taste quality, their sustainable and natural production system, and their strong links to the identity of the local culture. Although their product is symbolically and economically important, the producers of Canapu have never created an organization to represent their interests or to outline the production of Canapu to ensure a constant supply of good seed and to define the agricultural techniques that produce the best-quality cowpea.

The Presidium will respond to this need, starting in the small municipalities of Picos and Campogrande (Piauí State) and the production area will slowly broaden to include other areas. The objectives of the project include the organization of a nucleus of producers, the creation of a production protocol, and the promotion of the Canapu cowpea to a broader market. In the long term, the Presidium will encourage the formation of an association of producers.

This project was created thanks to a nomination from Embrapa and is being developed in collaboration with the Picos branch of Emater (Development Agency for the Piauí State), which is working directly to coordinate the producers involved.

Picos market (Piauí State)

**Production area**
Brazil
Piauí State

**Presidium Coordinator**
Gabrio Marinozzi
Tel. +55 61 426 9875
gabrio@terra.com.br

José Antonio de Sousa Batista (Emater)
Tel. +55 89 422 4453
emater-picos@emater.pi.gov.br

**Presidium supported by**
Mountain Community of Trasimeno-
Medio Tevere
Municipality of Corciano
Trasimeno Slow Food Convivium

**With the patronage of**
Brazilian Ministry of
Agricultural Development

The word 'bean' does not only refer to numerous species, varieties, and ecotypes, but also to two distinct botanical genera—the *Phaseolus* and the *Vigna*—from two distant continents, America and Africa.

Though they cannot be crossed, the two genera resemble each other from the morphological point of view and encompass extraordinary diversity: seeds are minuscule, enoromous, spotted or striped; plants are dwarfs or creepers; flowers white, pink, or violet; and harvest early or late.

The *Phaseolus* evolved in Central and South America in an area that included Mexico, Peru and Colombia, and was introduced into Europe by the Spanish and Portuguese *conquistadores*. Its wild ancestor was the *Phaseolus aborigineus*, a sturdy creeper with small black seeds. There are as many as 200 species of *Phaseolus*, but the most commonly cultivated are the following four: *Ph. vulgaris* (the most common), *Ph. coccineus* (Spanish bean), *Ph. lunatus* (Lima bean) and *Ph. acutifolius* (primarily grown in America, where it is known as the Tepary).

The *Vigna*, instead, is from Africa, Asia and Europe, and its wild progenitor was recently rediscovered in Nigeria. From south of the Sahara it spread in two directions, to the Far East and to the Mediterranean, both important centers of domestication. About

80 species exist, of which five or six are domesticated. The most important and common is the *Vigna unguiculata*.

The Americans have two words—'bean' (for *Phaseolus*) and 'cowpea' (for *Vigna*)—but the rest of the world makes no lexical

# Vigna Versus Phaseolus

distinction between the two genera.

Most beans currently produced worldwide are *Phaseolus*, as they are easier and more profitable to grow and yield almost double per hectare than *Vigna*.

Observing the plants, flowers, and seeds, technicians can easily tell the two genera apart, but the normal consumer cannot always distinguish between the two. The best way too tell is from the *Vigna*'s seeds, which have a marked ileum circled in black—hence their nickname, 'black-eyed peas'.

# Juçara
# Palm Heart

### The Palm's Crunchy Core

Brazil boasts an extraordinary amount of agricultural, gastronomic and cultural diversity. There are 210 indigenous groups living in the country who speak 18 languages. Guaraní is one of the most populous tribes and its members live in many Brazilian states, including Espírito Santo, São Paulo, Paraná, Santa Catarina, Rio Grande do Sul, and Mato Grosso do Sul.

The Guaraní are originally from Paraguay (according to their tradition, that country is the center of the world), where Guaraní is still the second language spoken. The identity of the Guaraní is tribal, rather than national, and is based on their language, religion and culture. Music and song unify the community and are considered divine manifestations.

Agriculture is based on the farming of sweet potatoes, manioc, corn and *palmito*, palm heart, from the trunk of the palm tree. The most traditional and flavorful variety of *palmito* comes from the Juçara (*Eutherpes edulis*), which grows naturally in the remaining portion of the Atlantic forest in southern Brazil. Juçara is also the variety most at risk. The *palmito* is extracted sustainably through the labor of the Guaraní Indians in only a few areas. Most palm hearts are removed by non-sustainable extraction methods carried out by non-Indian *palmeriteros* in the valleys of the Ribeira, one of the poorest regions of the state of São Paulo.

In the past few years, the Guaraní village of Rio Silveira in the Ribeira valleys has built a small nursery in the forest to help revive the native palm populations. The nursery is specialized in Juçara palms but also grows Jerivá Pindo Ovy, known as the

## The Presidium

The Presidium seeks to promote the *palmito* as a high quality product, giving added value to the Juçara Palm Heart. Before marketing the product, it is necessary to establish other restoration projects like those in the Boa Vista and Rio Silveira Reserves. With the help of the *Instituto Teko Arando*, an Indian organization, some 300 people work 948 hectares of land under the guidance of Adolfo Timótio, the head of the village, or *Verá Mirim Miri* in the Guaraní language. They are restoring the Juçara palm population by creating nurseries in the forest and by planting at least two new palms for every palm that is cut down. Wild birds and animals like toucans and rodents were once responsible for the dissemination of palm seeds and growth of new palms. The first steps of this project are designed to identify ways to cultivate and harvest the palms and educate local families in the hope of reinvigorating the Rio Silveira Reserve.

blue palm. The reforestation of the *mata atlântica* with these palms allows the Guaraní to slowly rebuild the numbers of their traditional palm.

The Juçara grows in the heart of the forest, requires little sunlight and no fertilizers or other treatment. The tree has a straight, thin, grayish-white trunk, which can grow as high as 15 meters. The tree must be at least eight to ten years old before the heart is removed by cutting off the top part of the trunk and the bark is stripped with a machete. Twice a year the seeds are gathered, usually by children, who are able to shimmy up the palm trunk with ease. Upon reaching the top of the tree, they pull off the large bunches of violet berries to expose the trunk and remove the heart.

The Juçara palm tree is used in its entirety: the leaves are used for making beds and chairs, the wood to build houses, and the berries to make an acidic juice. The Juçara Palm Heart is traditionally eaten raw with honey because there is no salt or sugar in Guaraní cuisine. It can also be boiled, roasted over an open fire or fried.

The Juçara palm is chopped down for sale and the heart is sold fresh on the spot or to a nearby restaurant. This precious and rare product can only be consumed after eight to ten years, when it is cut down and sold for the equivalent of a few dollars.

**Production Area**
Brazil
San Paolo State
Guaraní Reserves of Silveira
(Municipality of São Sebastião) and
Boa Vista (Municipality of Ubatuba)

**Producers**
50 families (250 individuals)

**Presidium Coordinators**
Gabrio Marinozzi
Tel. +55 (0) 61 426 9875
gabrio@terra.com.br

Maurício Fonseca
Tel. + 55 11 38153848
mafon@uol.com.br

**With the patronage of**
Brazilian Ministry of Agricultural
Development

# Sateré Mawé
# Native Guaranà

## Eyes in the Forest

Guaraná has been grown and harvested for thousands of years in Brazilian Amazonia by the Mawè indians, who call the tree Waranà. German botanist Christian Franz Paullini classified Guaraná in the eighteenth century as *Paullinia cupana* of the *Sorbilis* variety.

The Mawé do not 'farm' in the classic sense of the word; their system might best be called 'semi-domestication'. They collect the seeds that fall from Guaraná trees in the forest and plant them in clearings, where they are watered by the rain and tended minimally. In the forest, Guaraná can grow as high as 12 meters. The tree's white flowers grow in great long clusters in the shape of corn cobs. When the fruit ripens, it turns deep red and splits slightly to reveal a black seed in white flesh. The Mawé believe that the ripe fruit resembles an open eye. According to Mawé legend, the fruits are connected to a murdered child, whose eyeball, buried like a seed, grew into the Guaraná plant.

After the flesh of the ripe fruits is removed, the seeds are roasted for three days in terracotta ovens. The seeds are then shelled, pounded in a mortar, shaped into batons weighing from 150 grams to two kilos. These are packed in canvas bags and laid in the *fumeiros*, where they are smoked with aromatic wood.

The roasted Guaraná contains up to 5% caffeine and is rich in phosphorus, potassium, and other vitamins. The Mawé sustain that Guaraná revs up your nervous system, works against fatigue, stimulates cognitive functions and helps maintain energy during intense physical activity.

The powdered seeds can be dissolved in water, as happens in indigenous rituals, or can be diluted in fresh fruit juice. The fruit extract is used to make a variety of syrups and drinks such as *soda guaraná* (Brazil's national drink). Guaraná is also important in Mawé religious culture, where it has a symbolic role similar to that of wine in the Catholic liturgy.

## The Presidium

This Presidium has been established in collaboration with the Conselho Geral da Tribo Sateré Mawé (CGTSM), which brings together all of the indigenous families of the Sateré Mawé tribe to establish a production protocol that defines the traditional techniques of cultivation of Guaranà. In addition to conserving native Guaraná produced by the CGTSM, the Presidium will assist in developing and producing Guaraná syrups and other products for sale internationally.

For this project, Slow Food is collaborating with MLAL ProgettoMondo, a NGO for international cooperation active in Amazonia and CTM-Altromercato, which distributes native Guaraná to fair trade stores.

Photos Rémi Denecheau,, RDV Productions

### Slow Food's Accord with the Brazilian Goverment

Brazil's small landholders—those with just a few hectares of arable land—produce the vast majority of the country's food: 70% of beans, 58% of pork, 54% of beef, and 40% of eggs. These are surprising figures given that the majority of the country's 821 million hectares of farmland are owned by 1% of landowners. Given their numbers and high productivity, small farmers are the only real hope in fighting hunger and famine in Brazil. For this reason, even small projects like the Presidia are strategic both in rural development and in the battle against hunger and malnutrition.

In the month of July 2004 the Brazilian Minister and Vice-Ministers of Agricultural Development—respectively, Miguel Soldatelli Rossetto and Humberto Oliveira—and Slow Food President Carlo Petrini signed an important agreement, which marks the beginning of a collaboration to identify products at risk of extinction across Brazil. Given that the Agricultural Development Ministry is responsible precisely for the sector in which the Presidia operate—agricultural development in family-run farms and remote rural areas—this looks to be a fruitful collaboration. The first steps are four Presidia, among which Guaraná, all identified with the help of the Brazilian Ministry.

| Production Area | Producers | Presidium Coordinators | With the patronage of |
|---|---|---|---|
| Brazil | 450 Sateré Mawé families | Maurizio Fraboni | Brazilian Ministry of Agricultural |
| Amazonas and Pará States | | Tel. +55 92 6154763-88042688 | Development |
| Andirá-Marau Tribal Land | | acopiama@horizon.com.br | |
| | | | |
| | | Vanessa Gallo | |
| | | Acra-Icei Milano | |
| | | Tel. +39 02 27000291 | |
| | | vanessagallo@acra.it | |

# Umbu

## The Tree that Quenches Thirst

The Umbu (also known as *imbú*) is native to northeast Brazil, where it grows in the Caatinga, the chaparral scrub that grows wild across dry lands of the Sertão. The name of this tree and fruit comes from the indigenous phrase *y-mb-u*, which means 'tree that gives drink'. The productive cycle of this wild, spontaneously growing tree begins after ten years of growth. It bears fruit once a year and can produce up to 300 kilos of fruit in a single harvest when it reaches maturity. Due to its robust root system, a great network of tubers that can store liquid throughout the Sertão's dry season, the Umbu tree can hold up to 3,000 liters of water during the dry months.

This tree is an important resource for one of the poorest and driest regions of Brazil, where local agriculture is based on corn, beans, sheep, and goat (dried and salted goat meat is one of the most important local foods). The fruit of the Umbu tree is collected by hand—gently, as it is easily damaged—and during picking the fruits are set in baskets and bags (in the past these fruits were also collected by beating the branches with long poles, to the detriment of their flavor). The fruit of the Umbu are round and can be of varying size: they can be as small as cherries or as large as lemons. The peel is smooth and green or yellow when the fruit ripen, the small firm fruits are juicy and flavorful and their succulent flesh hides a large dark pit.

The Umbu can be eaten fresh or made into jams or other sweetened preserves like fruit cheese. In the Sertão, it is cooked down until the peel and the pulp separate. Then, the liquid is poured off, it is mixed with sugar and cooked for another two hours. After the pulp has been reduced to a glossy gelatin (called *geléia*), it retains a slightly astringent flavor. In addition to the thick paste made by this long, slow boiling process, the Umbu is the base of fruit juice, *vinagre* (the juice pressed from overripe fruit), and jam (made by pressing together layers of dried Umbu paste). Another delicacy is the compôte made by mixing the fruit and sugar together in jars. The fresh pulp, or—if the fresh fruit is not in season, the *vinagre*—is mixed with milk and sugar to make *umbuzada*, a rich beverage that is a common substitute for a full meal.

## The Presidium

Until a few years ago, no one paid much attention to this fruit. But the work of various organizations (the NGO IRPAA/PRO CUC, the KMB, the Austrian Lins diocese, and Austrian Horizon 3000) has improved the profile of Umbu. These groups have worked to improve the public reputation of Caatinga products and have followed the development of the COOPER-CUC cooperative, which produces products that have no added flavors or colors in a small workshop in Uauá in the state of Bahia.

The Presidium will draw up a production protocol that ensures the artisan quality of the products made from these fruits and raises the profile of the products on the national and international markets. The objectives extend beyond the improvement of the market for on-farm products to include the development of new work opportunities and new income, the protection of the environment, and the organizational potential of the local population, with a focus on jobs for women.

| Production Area | Producers | Presidium Coordinators | With the patronage of |
|---|---|---|---|
| Brazil<br>Bahia State<br>Sertão Bahiano Municipalities | 44 farmers united in the COPER-CUC Cooperative (under the leadership of Jussemar Cordeiro da Silva) | Gabrio Marinozzi<br>Tel. +55 (0) 61 426 9875<br>gabrio@terra.com.br<br><br>Erwin and Catharina Gross<br>PROCUC<br>Tel. +55 (0) 746731296<br>procuc@lkn.com.br | Brazilian Ministry of Agricultural Development |

Canada

# Red Fife Wheat

### The First on the Prairies

Red Fife Wheat was first grown in the Otonabee region of what is now central Ontario in the 1840s. A struggling farmer in the region, David Fife, planted Red Fife using seed samples from Scotland. Red Fife's striking similarities to the Halychanka wheat variety suggest that it is a descendant of this Ukrainian wheat. Others believe that what we call Red Fife was an accidental hybrid. Regardless of the exact origin, the few stalks of what came to be called Red Fife Wheat flourished as no other wheat had. Hardy and resistant to the diseases of the time, Red Fife also boasted exceptional flavor and baking properties that made it much in demand with farmers, millers and bakers. Its name derives from the farmer who introduced it and the deep color it achieves when fully ripe. The popularity of Red Fife continued to expand as increasing numbers of immigrants began to move across the Canadian Prairies in the early 1880s. The flat plains of rich soil were ideal for wheat growing and Red Fife provided farmers with a consistent, high quality crop in a harsh climate. According to Canadian government agronomists, the unique properties of Red Fife and its adaptation to the Canadian climate have made it the genetic parent to virtually all Canadian wheats grown on the prairies today.

Today, Red Fife has survived due to the work of only a handful of organic heritage wheat and seed farmers scattered across Canada who have been faithfully growing the wheat to keep it from extinction.

Artisan bread made from Red Fife Wheat has a hay yellow crumb, with an intense scent of herbs and vegetables colored with a light acidity. The nose has notes of anise and fennel, and in the mouth the bread is unexpectedly rich with a slightly herby and spicy flavor.

### Genetically Modified Wheat: Coming Soon to Canada?

For the past three years, organic farmer Marc Loiselle has led a crusade to protect Canadian farmers against the potential economic losses related to the cultivation of GM crops with a class action lawsuit against Monsanto. He represents 500 Saskatchewan farmers, and his suit asks that Monsanto be obliged to cover financial losses from the contamination of non-GM crops with GM genes. Canadians farm over ten million hectares of wheat, and according to the Canadian Wheat Board, almost 90% of Canadian wheat buyers abroad want their wheat GM-free.

"Given the Canadian and Saskatchewan reliance on the export of wheat and other crops, the class action suit targets the vulnerability of this export market if it is contaminated by GM varieties," explains Loiselle. This is a lesson taken from the experiences of Canadian farmers after the introduction of GM canola stock: today the contamination is so diffuse because of cross-pollination that it is impossible to certify that any Canadian canola is GM-free.

In May 2004, the Monsanto Company announced its deferral of the introduction of GM wheat indefinitely, partially in response to consumer campaigns around the globe. Yet, Loiselle remains firm in insisting that Monsanto's deferral is not enough. Most agree with Loiselle that, if not this year, four or five years from now Monsanto's campaign to introduce commercial cultivation of GM wheat varieties will continue.

### The Presidium

Red Fife wheat, Canada's first Presidium, seeks to bring Red Fife wheat back into commercial circulation for use in artisan bread baking. In the first year of activity, the Presidium has involved five farmers in growing the wheat to increase seed stock and make commercial production possible. The taste quality of handmade bread from Red Fife flour has been promoted through an 'Artisan Bread Tour' in six Canadian cities. The Presidium has petitioned the Canadian Wheat Board for legal recognition of the variety, a campaign that could lead to more widespread cultivation of Red Fife Wheat in the Canadian Prairies.

| Production Area | Producers | Presidium Coordinator |
|---|---|---|
| Canada<br>Central Ontario and Provinces of Alberta, Saskatchewan and Manitoba | Five farmers and a baker | Mara Jernigan<br>Tel. +1 250 7434267<br>engeler@telus.net |

# Blue Egg Chicken

## The Unusual Araucana

In the area surrounding the Chilean city of Temuco, farmers' market stalls are laden with the kaleidoscopic displays of eggs colored cobalt blue, pale green, and everything in between. Temuco is particularly famous for its blue eggs. While most farm-raised chickens lay the occasional blue egg, Temuco chickens always lay blue or green eggs, a genetic trait that turns the bird's white eggs blue and its brown eggs green. In Chile, this particular chicken breed is called the Araucana, the name that conquering Spaniards gave the Mapuche people, as well as to the region's chickens, ultimately. It is unclear whether the Araucana chicken is an indigenous breed or if it is a descendant of the chickens first brought from Spain by the *conquistadores*.

The Araucana has been the subject of much interest and research in Chile, and apparently it is unique in its ability to exclusively produce blue eggs. Many of the breeds now present in the Americas that regularly produce a percentage of blue eggs may well be descended from crosses with the Araucana.

Today, the Araucana has been crossed with so many different breeds that it is no longer possible to describe it as a 'pure' breed with predictable physical characteristics. Historical documents describe Chilean native chicken breeds as being divided into two main categories: the *colloncas*, with a short rear end and no feathers around the ears, and *quetros*, with a normal profile and a fully feathered head. More likely than not, the chickens with short rear ends are of Asian origin and were brought to Chile by Dutch traders from Bali. Physically speaking, the Araucana appears to be part of the *colloncas* type, but the blue egg characteristic is nonexistent in Balinesian chickens, and appears to have been a mutation in the imported chickens upon their arrival and selection in southern Chile. To fully understand the Araucana, long and complicated research is necessary, together with selection within the various chicken populations. Even then, as with many animal breeds that are poorly documented and frequently crossed, the Araucana will always have a mysterious past.

Although the laying chickens all have different physical appearances, they are clearly from the wide gene pool of the Araucana, and none can survive in industrial chicken farms. These chickens must be kept outside in order to produce eggs. In Chile, where agriculture is rapidly intensifying, the blue eggs are a uniquely valuable 'self-identifying' product: the eggshells themselves are a sign of free-range quality and one that cannot be counterfeited.

### The Presidium

Slow Food's partner in this Presidium is Temuco NGO CET SUR, which has worked for years to promote traditional Mapuche foods and blue eggs as healthy and natural products. The Presidium will support the research and selection of the historic Araucana breed. To this end, the Presidium will work with the network of small farmers, *Curadoras de semillas*, Chilean Seed Savers, which is widespread in southern Chile and considered an important protector of vegetable and animal diversity, working to save local species such as medicinal herbs, black quinoa, and local potato varieties. The *curadoras* will raise groups of Blue Egg Chicken, sell them on the national market, and collaborate on research and selection efforts coordinated by the Presidium.

**Production Area**
Chile
Bio Bio and Araucania Regions

**Producers**
12 breeders united in *Curadoras de Semillas*

**Presidium Coordinators**
Max Thomet (NGO CET SUR)
Tel. +56 45 248835
mthomet@cetsur.org

Francisco Klimscha
Slow Food Convivium Leader
Tel. +56 99 198471
slowfoodchile@hotmail.com

# Farmers
# by Necessity

Around 800-700 BCE, a tribe believed to be related to the Brazilian Guaranì crossed the Andes and settled in Chile, from the Atacama deserts of the north down to the cold southern deserts of Chiloè. These Mapuche—which means 'people of the earth' in their language—lived for centuries as hunter-gatherers and fishermen, ranging over great areas of land. The Mapuche learned to defend their rights and became tenacious warriors.

The Mapuche's social structure, based upon the family, or *ruca*, including all male descendants with their wives and children, tends to create constant strife between various clans. However, this hostility ceased with the presence of outside threats, when all clans elected a *gran toqui*, or military chief, and banded together against the enemy. The conquest of the Incas stopped at the Bio Bio river, border of the Mapuche land, and they called them the Auca, meaning 'disobedient', 'savage' and 'rebellious'. Even the Spanish failed to conquer this tribe: southern Chile was the only South American territory to resist the *conquista*. On the first of January, 1554, the Mapuche routed the Spanish troops, capturing and executing the Spanish commanding officer, Captain General Pedro Valdivia. The Mapuche recognize this date as the beginning of their independence. Only through the firm determination of the Chilean government and fifteen years of war, using methods that invoked mentions of

A Mapuche family photographed in 1993 on the Bio Bio river, photo by Chris Rainier, Corbis/Contrasto

genocide in the press, did Colonel Cornello Saavedra succeed in annexing the nation of the Mapuche into the Chilean state in 1881. It was not an easy process; for years local resistance persisted, but the harshest repression continued. The most disastrous effect of this war was the deprivation of the Mapuche (or Araucani, as they were called by the Spanish) of their traditional methods of sustenance. They were forced into small rural areas, their mountain passes were closed and their animals taken away. The elders of the tribe said in the beginning of the twentieth century, "First we were warriors and they make us into sowers." This change was dramatic, particularly because the population had no real agricultural tradition; they were forced to adapt at the price of a great decline in their quality of life and cultural pride. Consequent Chilean governments continued the persecution—the worst under Pinochet, who claimed to see seeds of communism in their social structure. Irenes Weche, a *mochi*, or spiritual guide, from Temuco says, "It was a great time of celebration for the Mapuche when Pinochet lost." In fact, this population, considered the dictatorship's greatest enemies, suffered the most under his regime.

# Calbuco Black-Bordered Oyster

## Wild Oysters
## South of Santiago

If you drive 1,200 kilometers south of Santiago, you arrive at the small port of Calbuco, off of which families of tenacious small fishermen still populate a large archipelago. About an hour after leaving the port in a small wooden boat you reach the island of Chiduapi. The landscape of the island's 114 hectares is reminiscent of that of Scotland: woodland, emerald green pastures, sheep, wooden houses looking out to sea, a church, a small school, a cemetery, and little else. It is a beautiful spot, without hotels, restaurants, shops, electricity, or telephones. On Chiduapi, rare days of sunshine are squeezed between rain and freezing wind. Here, the tradition of catching wild oysters has been passed down for at least four generations. During the twice-daily low tides, the water in the island's bays retreats as far as 300 meters, leaving the oyster beds uncovered. The fishermen go out at low tide, select the largest oysters and bring them near the shore. Here, there are simple stone enclosures for holding oysters selected for sale. The enclosures are marked off by nets fitted with white buoys, which allow divers to gather the oysters at high tide. Calbuco Black-Bordered Oysters are smaller than those found in other parts of the world—where they are cultivated in clusters suspended in the water—but offer better taste and texture and can easily be distinguished by their distinctive black fringe when opened.

## The Presidium

The technique of gathering wild oysters on Chiduapi is disappearing: the number of gatherers can be counted on one hand. This ancient system respects the natural cycle of oyster beds by limiting harvesting to just six months of the year, in autumn and winter, when oysters do not reproduce, and selecting the largest specimens which are at least three years old.

This Presidium has been set up to help the last fishermen of the islands strengthen their organization and create a marketable name to distinguish their Black-Bordered Oyster from others. This will secure a distinct market, rewarding a product with excellent taste qualities, as wild oysters and cultivated oysters are currently sold at the same price on the Chilean market, as well as preserving a traditional and sustainable fishing practice. The Presidium will also help encourage the improvement of the infrastructure on Calbuco to support commercialization of the archipelago's sustainably fished products.

**Production Area**
Chile
Calbuco Archipelago

**Producers**
Three families of fishermen

**Presidium Coordinators**
Francisco Klimscha
Slow Food Convivium Leader
Tel. +56 99198471
slowfoodchile@hotmail.com

Alejandro Soto Velasquez
Tel. +56 29465038

On Chiduapi, the traditional island clambake, or *curanto*, is more a ritual than a meal. To prepare the *curanto*, the fishermen dig a hole and carefully lay stones side by side in the bottom—tiling the baking pit. Then, a fire is lit on top of the stones and burned down until just coal and embers remain. Local *nalca* leaves are used to line the pit in which the fishermen stack a thick layer of crustaceans and mollusks.

*Piures,* coral red shellfish with a strong iodine flavor, go in first. Then the *picorocos,* a thick crustacean that looks like a giant barnacle with three or four long tentacles, is layered on. Next mussels of varying sizes are piled on: the smallest are called *choritos,* the medium sized ones *malton,* and the biggest—the size of a fist—*choro zapatos.*

The fishermen add a sprinkling of clams, or *almejas,* to the top. The final layer of the deep *curanto* is meat: sausage, pork cutlets and loin, as well as a good layer of potatoes, skin and all.

This inverted mountain of roasting shellfish, pork, and potatoes is covered with aromatic branches of *arallan* and *nalca* leaves, then dotted with flat pancakes made of grated raw potatoes, flour, and butter, or *chapalele.* The clambake is covered with a thick cloth weighed down with earth and sand. After an hour and a half, the *curanto* is ready.

*Curanto* is not simply a dish, but a real convivial ritual, which celebrates the rare days of sunshine that darken into cold night here at the extreme south of the southern hemisphere.

# Convivial Curanto

# Merken

## Chile and Coriander Season Temuco

Pablo Neruda describes the Temuco of his childhood as 'a pioneering city, without a past but with hardware shops.' Modernization has changed this image of the city, but a visit to the town market still makes you feel as if you are in a border zone. Temuco is chaotic and full of colorful merchandise, partly because it is home to the highest concentration anywhere of Mapuche Indians, who come to the market to trade and sell their blue eggs, hand-made fabrics, traditional musical instruments, Araucana chickens and Merken. The bags and bags of Merken fill the air with sweet and spicy aromas.

Merken, a spice mixture, is made primarily of a long, pointed chili pepper called *aji*, or *caciocavra* in local dialect. The pepper is grown throughout the region and is gathered in February, when it turns from bright green to red. After the harvest, the *caciocavra* is sun-dried until it becomes violet-colored. The dried chilies are smoked for half an hour and are hung from the ceiling in wicker baskets directly over a wood-fire. After being dried in the sun a second time, the *aji* is finely ground, first with a stone mortar, then in an automatic grinder. Lightly smoked coriander seeds and sea salt are added to the *aji* powder. Merken is always made with at least 70% chili powder and never more than 20% salt. The spice is used to flavor soups, meats, omelettes and salads and was always found on the table in Chilean homes. Today, for new generations of Chileans, Merken represents a past of poverty and is an expression of the part of Indian culture that they are trying to forget.

## The Presidium

The Presidium was founded, in collaboration with the local NGO CET SUR, to reintroduce Merken into the local diet. The Presidium version of the spice must be made according to the authentic recipe, which calls for coriander and not cumin, with a modicum of salt. The Presidium will promote the production of Merken in traditional areas, to encourage the Mapuche to cultivate *caciocavra* and cilantro and the few spice-makers to use local ingredients. The spice will also be brought to the attention of the top restaurateurs in Chile and South America to be used both in traditional dishes and new, creative recipes.

**Production Area**
Chile
Region IX
Municipality of Temuco

**Producers**
Twelve artisans

**Presidium Coordinators**
Max Thomet (NGO CET SUR)
Tel. +56 45 248835-45 248796
mthomet@cetsur.org

Francisco Klimscha
Slow Food Convivium Leader
Tel. +56 99198471
slowfoodchile@hotmail.com

# Purén White Strawberries

## The Modern Strawberry's White Ancestor

White strawberries have existed for centuries in central southern Chile around the small community of Purén. This strangely colorless fruit cultivated between the Cordigliera and the Pacific gave rise to all the world's strawberries. Large modern strawberries actually have a relatively recent history, dating back to the nineteenth century, whereas the fruit that was documented before the discovery of the New World—by Pliny, Virgil, and Ovid—are these tiny *Fragaria vesca*, or forest strawberries.

In 1614 the Spanish missionary Alfonso Ovalle discovered large strawberries in the countryside near the city of Concepcion, which were then classified as *Fragaria chiloensis*, known commonly as Chilean strawberries. In 1712 Francois Frezier, an engineer in the service of Louis XIV, brought some specimens to Europe, and only five plants survived the six-month sea voyage. Modern strawberries were born in Brest, France, in 1766, from a cross between the *Fragaria virginiana* of the eastern United States and the white *chiloensis*.

This first hybrid, called *Fragaria ananassa*, was then crossed and crossed again to create the large red varieties grown today. The Chilean white strawberry is rotund with a small point and pale flesh, sometimes just barely tinged pink, but more often ivory with points of rose or red. It is cultivated around Purén, particularly in the Manzanal, an area removed from the Cordigliera Nahualbuta that faces the sea.

The fields are steep and cut away from the forest. Twenty-five farmers work some fourteen hectares of poor clay terrain without tractors, irrigation or fertilizer.

The harvest begins at the end of November and continues until mid-January. Here, white strawberries are eaten during Christmas and New Year's like mandarin oranges in Europe and North America.

## The Presidium

Purén White Strawberries are sold directly by the producers in the fields or at local markets and fairs. They are never served in a local restaurant or even in city establishments. The Presidium was formed in collaboration with the city of Purén to spread knowledge and appreciation for this fruit. Through a series of initiatives, Slow Food Chile is promoting the strawberries in restaurants all around Chile, especially in Santiago, where an event has already been planned for Christmas of 2004. The production protocol, which ensure that the origins of this fruit are documented, will be completed with the help of Comite da Pequeños Agricultores de Frutilla Blanca.

**Production Area**
Chile
Region IX
Municipality of Purén

**Producers**
25 farmers united in the *Comité de Pequeños Agricultores de Frutilla Blanca*

**Presidium Coordinators**
Roberto Giacomozzi
Tel. +56 99699187-45 793344
rgiacomo1@hotmail.com
www.frutillablancadepuren.cl

Francisco Klimscha
Slow Food Convivium Leader
Tel. +56 99198471
slowfoodchile@hotmail.com

# Robinson Crusoe
# Island Seafood

## A Rainbow Undersea

It takes two and a half hours by plane from Santiago, half an hour on foot, and an hour by boat to reach the lone tiny village on the island of Robinson Crusoe in the Juan Fernandez archipelago.

The name of this island is linked to the incredible adventures of Alexander Selkirk, made legendary in Daniel Defoe's novel, and somehow the island still retains an evocative atmosphere. Landing on the airstrip is an adventure in itself, as the plane coasts to a stop in a desert-like landscape. In the distance the plaintive cries of gulls and seals can be heard as they float serenely in the water. A boat takes you round to the other side of the island into a lush world of woods, streams and pastures reminiscent of high altitude meadows. 83% of animal and plant species on this island are indigenous, including native species of seaweed, birds and mammals and, in particular, fish and shellfish. Goats and wild rabbits live in inland areas and a few cattle are farmed, but the real life on the island is found in the sea. Almost all the island's inhabitants have fished for a living for at least three centuries. The most celebrated catch, which dates back to at least 1700, is the local rock lobster. This species, *Jasus frontalis*, is found only here and in the waters of the Desventuradas Islands of San Felix and Sant'Ambrosio, a three-hour boat trip to the north.

The lobsters are caught at a depth of 50 to 100 meters by lowering rectangular traps made by the fishermen from the branches of the local *maqui* tree. Until a few years ago the traps would be lifted by hand; a small motor is now used—the only concession to innovation. The small wooden boats are based on the design of old whaling ships and have historically been built on the island by the

There are many fish, mollusks and shellfish of gastronomic interest found in the waters around the islands, but only the rock lobster has been used to date. Excellent fish such as the sea bream are simply used as bait.

This Presidium was established to protect a unique ecosystem and exceptional example of exclusively artisan fishing. The aim is to make the island's fish resources more widely known, without focusing solely on lobster fishing, which, in spite of present limitations on catching season and size over the long term, risks compromising stock levels.

The Presidium also hopes to create a marine reserve banning industrial fishing vessels from entering these waters.

Chamorro family.

Lobster fishing on Robinson Crusoe Island is only allowed between October and mid-May and the specimens caught must be at least 12 to 14 years old.

The waters of the island have many other species of interesting fish, mollusks and shellfish of gastronomic interest, such as the red crab (*Geryon quinquedens*), which is caught at a depth of five to six hundred meters using the same wooden cages as the rock lobster, the black sea urchin (*Aspidodiadema microtuberculatum*), and the sea bream (*Cheilodactylus gayi*), a fish with fine white flesh, caught with a very long hook called an *espinel*.

**Production Area**
Chile
Juan Fernandez Archipelago
Robinson Crusoe Island

**Producers**
84 fishermen united in the *Sindicato de trabajadores independientes de pescadores artesanales del Archipiélago de Juan Fernández*

**Presidium Coordinators**
Francisco Klimscha
Slow Food Convivium Leader
Tel. +56 99198471
slowfoodchile@hotmail.com

Hugo Arredondo Schiller
Tel. +56 32751115

# Nacional Cacao

## Chocolate from 'Gran Cacao'

In the 1820s, Simon Bolivar carved the Republic of Gran Colombia out of the lands his armies had liberated from colonial rule in Latin America. Composed of the territory that has become modern-day Venezuela, Colombia, Panama and Ecuador, the Republic was nicknamed 'Gran Cacao' after its most famous product.

The plantations of 'Gran Cacao'—especially those in Venezuela and Ecuador—were the chief exporters of cacao to Europe for some 300 years. In the early nineteenth century, Ecuador produced over 30% of the world's cacao with almost 60 million planted trees, almost all of which were of the Nacional variety.

A century ago, most of Ecuador's arable land was planted with cacao, but landowners gradually began to grow other crops such as sugar cane, bananas, and coffee. Two devastating diseases infected cacao trees in the early 1920s, almost destroying production and leading to the substitution of millions of acres of Nacional trees with more disease-resistant hybrids.

Nacional Cacao is a descendant of the cacao trees first developed and cultivated by the Mayans in South America. It is an exceptionally flavorful and delicate cacao type, found only in Ecuador—hence its patriotic name. Genetically, the Nacional is a Forastero cacao, but the flavor and aroma of the chocolate it produces are similar to those usually associated with the legendary Criollo cacao. Forastero, of the subspecies *Theobroma cacao sphaerocarpum*, tends to be a robust plant that matures quickly and produces a rougher chocolate than Criollo beans.

Napo Province, a center of production of Nacional Cacao today, is at the heart of the Ecuadorian Amazon. Its population is almost totally indigenous: the Quichua tribe is in the majority and the Quijos and

## The Presidium

The Nacional Cacao Presidium has been created with the Napo Province's Kallari Cooperative in response to the diminishing number of productive Nacional trees left in Ecuador. Its aim is to assist the indigenous cacao farming communities in the fermentation and drying of their cacao beans and help them obtain better prices.

In addition, the recent discovery of oil reserves in the area of the cacao-producing communities of Napo Province and the potential extraction of that oil by large international companies pose a serious environmental risk. The Quichua farmers of the Kallari Cooperative Association are working to prove to the Ecuadorian government that cacao production represents a viable alternative to oil concessions to foreign companies. For the Quichua, cacao could serve as a cash crop and at the same time provide enormous benefits in terms of the environmental conservation of the region. The Kallari Cooperative promotes greater agricultural diversity and better economic opportunities for more communities in the region through the expansion of sustainable cacao production.

Robert Steinberg, director and co-founder of Scharffen Berger, a noted American chocolate maker, first proposed this project. Steinberg, the project's Technical Partner, will work in the upcoming months with the Presidium project to develop a Nacional-based chocolate and to consult on the technical improvement of chocolate quality.

Chibcha tribes are in the minority. The area's physical remoteness has contributed to cultural isolation (even today the only way to travel to the province's capital city of Tena is by bus on a bumpy dirt road from Quito). This isolation has protected Ecuador's last stands of Nacional trees, which flourish in the Quichua villages deep in the Amazonian forest. While in other parts of the country it has been replaced by higher-yielding and disease-resistant hybrid varieties, in the Quichua villages of Napo, Nacional remains the primary variety.

| Production Area | Producers | Presidium Coordinator | Presidium supported by |
|---|---|---|---|
| Ecuador | 350 families united in the Kallari | Judy Logback | Eurochocolate |
| Napo Province | Cooperative | Tel. +593 22 453 583 | |
| Quichua villages around the | | kallari@jatunsacha.org | |
| Municipality of Tena | **Technical Partner** | | |
| | Scharffen Berger Chocolate Maker | | |

## Guatemala

# Huehuetenango Coffee

### Five 'Cru' Coffees

Jesuit priests introduced coffee to Guatemala in 1773 and today the country produces some of the finest coffee in the world. Huehuetenango, at the foot of the Cuchumatanes, one of the highest non-volcanic mountain ranges in Central America, is one of the best regions in Guatemala for coffee production. In Huehuetenango, currents of hot air sweeping up from the isthmus of Tehuatepec cross paths with cool air descending from the Cuchumatanes Mountains, and this unusual climactic situation allows the cultivation of coffee, unique for the quality of its beans, flavor and aroma, at altitudes up to 1,900 meters. Huehuetenango is in the northwest of Guatemala, on the border with Mexico. It is primarily a mountainous region, with altitudes ranging from 850 to 3,700 meters, though the region has an extraordinary variety of ecosystems (from subtropical forest to pine thickets).

The indigenous population, the majority of the local inhabitants, descends from various Maya tribes, including the Mam, the Akatecas, the Chuj, the Q'anjobal, and the Jacaltecas, each of which has a distinct language and culture. Their historic isolation from the Guatemalan population and the recent crisis in international coffee prices have made the indigenous inhabitants of Huehuetenango among the poorest in Central America. The recent collapse in coffee prices has thus caused a similar collapse in the local economy. The only means of escaping this vicious circle is through diversification: developing high-end niche-market coffees and introducing other products (hot peppers, anise, vegetables) in areas that are not well adapted to coffee. The Presidium coffee is made from plants of *Coffea arabica* (of the Typica, Bourbon and Caturra varieties) cultivated in the shade of the forest. The coffee berries are hand-harvested, picked one by one and placed in a wicker basket tied round the harvester's waist with a vine cord. The beans are extracted from the berries with a gentle fermentation that begins no more than four hours after harvest and lasts 24 to 36 hours. After removal of the coffee berry's flesh, the beans are dried for at least three hours, during which time they are constantly turned manually with a wooden rake.

## The Presidium

The Presidium began with eight cooperatives of producers coordinated by the local ASDECOHUE and ACODIHUE development agencies, which drew up a production protocol outlining coffee production at above 1,500 meters. A mapping of the production area has shown that there are five zones particularly suited for coffee production. In order to improve the quality of coffee production here, the producers are working constantly with technical assistance, especially with the fermentation of the beans. Given their dedicated effort to improve quality, it is important to reward producers with better prices for their coffee, and for this reason the Presidium is working to promote the product with reliable roasters and vendors.

Two projects related to the commercialization of the coffee directly involve the growers. In Huehuetenango, the Presidium is collaborating with the European Union, the Austrian government, NGO MAIS (Movimiento para el Autodesarollo Intercambio y Solidaridad) and I3W (Iniziative fur Dritte Welt) to build a center to process and roast beans. In Italy, a coffee roaster will be built in the Le Vallette prison in Turin. This last project will involve producers from Huehuetenango, a group of prisoners and local coffee roasters. For more information on the prison project, contact info@caffehuehuetenango.org.

### Production Area
Guatemala
Western *altipiano* of Huehuetenango
Municipalities of San Pedro Necta, La Libertad, Cuilco, La Democracia and Todos Santos Cuchumatanes

### Producers
Over 100 coffee growers that are part of eight cooperatives united in the umbrella organization of ASDECOHUE (Director, Daniel Palacios) and ACODIHUE (Director, Mariano Suasnavar)

Two Italian coffee roasters are promoting the Huhuetenango coffee Presidium crus: Torrefazione Caffè Del Doge (www.caffedeldoge.com) and Trinci (www.impressioni.it)

### Presidium Coordinators
Marco Ferrero (MAIS)
Tel. +39 011 19711488
marzia_sica@hotmail.com

Manrique Lopez Castillo
Tel. +502 7643103
mlopez@guatemais.org

# Chinantla Vanilla

## Where Vanilla Grows Wild

The hot and humid forest of Chinantla, a region in the state of Oaxaca just over 100 kilometers from the Gulf of Mexico, provides a perfect environment for growing vanilla. Already in the fifteenth century, precious vanilla from Chinantla was paid in tribute to Aztec emperor Montezuma, and its name in the local language, *kuo li gm*, dates back to that time. Then, vanilla was more valued as a fragrance than a spice and was used by Aztec women to scent oil pressed from seeds and to dress their hair.

Vanilla farming fell into neglect in the nineteenth century and was only revived in the 1990s as an alternative to coffee farming, which provided the vast majority of—unreliable—income to local farmers. Chinantla is the only region in the world where vanilla grows wild, as well as the area with the species' greatest genetic diversity. Here, five or six different varieties have been identified, though not all have been fully documented. This genetic diversity and the presence of wild vanilla plants suggest that Chinantla could be the area in which vanilla first originated.

The scientific name of the vanilla plant, an orchid, is *Vanilla planifolia*, but it's known locally as *colibrí*. In Chinantla, vanilla vines are cultivated in forests where they grow on and up citrus and banana plants or on local trees like Honduras Mahogany, known as Caoba. Vanilla leaves are long, thick, silky, and dark green, and the flowers sprout off the vine in bunches, like those on a grape vine.

Vanilla blossoms contain both male and female organs. A fine membrane divides the flower's stigma from its rostellum and must be lifted by hand, while the flower is gently pressed to pollinate the blossom. This delicate operation is carried out in the early hours of the morning in the beginning of May. For every large bunch of flowers, just three or four flowers are pollinated, since the fewer seedpods that form the higher their quality. The fresh vanilla bean is meaty and bright green, grows up to 15-25 centimeters long, and contains thousands of tiny seeds.

Straight after the harvest, the vanilla beans are dried for six to eight hours at around 65°C, then laid out in the sun for two months. Chinantla vanilla is finely scented and the beans are soft and flexible with a deep brown coffee color.

## The Presidium

This Presidium began in Rancho Grande, a small agricultural network that includes around 200 farmers coordinated by agronomist Raúl Manuel Antonio. Antonio has developed various small agricultural development systems that produce high-quality foods such as coffee and vanilla. Antonio received the Slow Food Award in 2000, Rancho Grande has become a model for many groups of farmers. The Presidium is working specifically with farmers from the towns of Cerro Verde and Flor Batavia, although the project will expand to include farmers from Arroyo Tambor and San Felipe Usila. The primary goal is to document and improve the production of vanilla.

In 2004, work on the production protocol began and a small group of farmers (they call themselves the 'Forest Guardians') agreed to follow a series of self-imposed guidelines to improve quality and reduce impact on the forest. The Presidium producers are participating in a series of theoretical and practical courses coordinated by experts Elías García Martínez, Teatinos Martínez Velasco and Longino Tenorio Mendoza.

The Presidium is also working to identify the various varieties of vanilla with the help of the Veracruz Center for Tropical Studies (CITRO), led by biologist Arturo Gómez-Pompa. For techinical assistance, the Presidium is collaborating with the Agropecuario No.3 Technical Institute in Tuxtepec.

**Production Area**
Mexico
Oaxaca State
Municipalities of San Felipe Usila, San Juan Bautista, Valle Nacional, San Andrés Teutila, San Andrés Teotilapan, and San Pedro Ixcatlán

**Producers**
65 families of producers united in three communities: Rancho Grande, Cerro Verde, and Flor Batavia

**Technical Partner**
Baiocco A. & Figlio (Italy)

**Presidium Coordinator**
Elías García Martínez
Tel. +52 2878753681
elias_garciam@hotmail.com

**Presidium supported by**
Region of Sicily
Regional Ministry of Agriculture and Forestry

Mexico

# Criollo Corn

76

## On the Chiapas *Altipiano*

7,000 years ago the wild corn plant was domesticated in Mexico. Corn's wild ancestors produced a few tiny bitter ears on each stalk—each ear grew just an inch-and-a-half long—but after thousands of years of selection, corn has been developed into many varieties that turn out sweet, juicy ears that can grow over a foot long.

Corn can be grown at sea level and up to an altitude of 9,000 feet. Today it remains one of the primary sources of carbohydrates in the Mexican diet. In Mexico City alone, Mexicans consume over 600 million corn tortillas a day. Many traditional foods are made from corn: *atole*, a thick drink; tacos, fried stuffed tortillas; *pastel azteca*, a type of lasagna layered with corn tortillas; and *tamales*, grits stuffed with meat or vegetables, wrapped in corn husks and steamed.

Corn has an important role in Hispanic and pre-Hispanic culture, and according to *Popol Vuh*, the creation story of Mayan culture, man was born from a sheaf of corn.

Mayan farmers probably selected many of the corn types seen in Mexico today. These local varieties have white, yellow, red and blue kernels; each type of corn has a slightly different flavor, consistency and color. Notwithstanding the historical significance of the ancient varieties, highly productive hybrid (and at times genetically modified) corn varieties that require abundant fertilizer, insecticide, and irrigation now dominate Mexico's cornfields. The price of corn is dropping as the market is flooded with inexpensive imports from North America. In the land where corn was first selected as a food crop, 35–40% of corn consumed is imported from the United States.

This Presidium promotes *criollo* (native) corn varieties in the Los Altos region of Chiapas. The long-term objective of the Presidium is to extend the growing area to include other parts of Mexico.

In Los Altos, the majority of the population (70%) is indigenous, and you are more likely to hear people speaking Tzeltal and Tzotzil than Spanish. The marginalization of the indigenous population in this area is acute. Nearly half of the population is illiterate, and many of the houses, patched together out of scavenged hay, bamboo, reeds, palms, mud, bricks, and cardboard, lack electricity, running water, and septic systems.

## The Presidium

This Presidium (or *spojel ixim* in the local language) has been developed in the very region where native Mexicans first began to struggle for their independence and liberty. There are numerous objectives for the project in Chiapas: the conservation of the system of the *milpa*, a traditional mixed farming technique where corn is planted alongside beans; the revival of local corn varieties; the organization of farmers; the improvement of production; and the promotion of the native Criollo Corn in restaurants and *tortillerías* and among consumers.

Presidium producers have experimented with the use of organic sheep manure as fertilizer and other natural methods of cultivation. Visits have also been organized by the Presidium producers to Teopisca to see the other organic cultivation systems used by different communities. The Presidium has invested in a Nissan pick-up to facilitate connections between the companies involved in the Presidium and has constructed a communal warehouse in Oventic.

The various phases of the project have been concluded, and now Slow Food is taking a step back to wait for the producers to take the lead on commercializing their local corn. Given the region's central Zapatista authority's stance on travel, producers are not allowed to leave Chiapas for security reasons and therefore cannot participate in international events like Terra Madre or the Salone del Gusto, and extensive promotion is thus impossible. But clear steps have been made towards development, and above all, this Presidium will work to raise awareness among the indigenous community about the importance of its traditional products.

**Production Area**
Mexico
Los Altos del Chiapas
Municipalities of San Andrés Larrainzar, Chenalhó, Teopisca, Amatenango del Valle and Nicolás Ruiz

**Producers**
5,000 farmers in 50 communities

**Presidium Coordinators**
Enlace Civil
Tel. +51 967 82104
enlacecivil@laneta.apc.org

Luca Fabbri
Tel. +39 329 9079007
luca.fabbri3@bcc.tin.it

# Tehuacán
# Amaranth

## From Mexico's Pre-Columbian Past

Corn, beans, and amaranth were the fundamentals of the diet of pre-Hispanic peoples from Mexico down to Peru. Yet unlike corn and beans, which have remained mainstays of the South American diet, amaranth has been almost completely abandoned. Important for its nutritional properties and ability to survive in the most arid regions, this resistant crop has been rediscovered in the last thirty years.

The *Amaranthus hypocondriacus* plant originated in the Tehuacán Valley (where it was domesticated between 5200 and 3400 BCE), and it can reach two to three meters in height. It has large green leaves and magnificent flowers: brilliantly colored plumes of deep red with touches of green and salmon pink.

Due to its beauty, amaranth used to be widely used for celebrations and religious rituals, including some particularly cruel ones, which provoked Christian missionaries to ban its cultivation. Five hundred years after it was abandoned, a slow but significant effort to revive its use and reintroduce some amaranth varieties has had some success. Amaranth can enrich the poor diet of many native people in Central and South America as it is rich in protein (particularly lysine, a key amino acid involved in growth processes). Amaranth can be eaten as a vegetable and the leaves are richer in iron than spinach, which makes it an ideal addition to a young person's diet. It can also be eaten in salads and soups or dried and used as a spice. Toasted Amaranth seeds are used to make traditional sweet food such as *alegría* in Mexico. Alternatively, flour can be produced for making tortillas (mixed with corn flour of course), cakes and cookies. In addition, like buckwheat, amaranth belongs to the category of minor cereals that do not contain gluten and for this reason can be used to make bread, pasta and cookies for people with celiac disease.

## Amaranth at the University of Milan

A group of researchers at the Food Science Department of the University of Milan, the primary Italian center of research in the field, is working with the Molecular Studies of Food and Agriculture Department of the same university, the Sant'Angelo Lodigiano Experimental Cericulture Institute and the Slow Food Foundation to develop new possibilities for the Tehuacán Amaranth Presidium. The goal of the collaboration is to commercialize amaranth and it is financed by the Cariplo Foundation.

Dr. Maria Lucisano, the project director, is specialized in cereal production and processing and recently has begun to focus on minor cereals like buckwheat and quinoa. This program will develop two lines of promotion for these minor cereals. First off, they will work to develop breads, cereals and cookies based on wheat and amaranth. Then, the research team will work with Slow Food in producing innovative products for celiacs (who cannot tolerate gluten), a rapidly expanding market, which could permit the number of Presidium producers to increase.

At the end of the experimental phase, Slow Food will evaluate the final products made. All of the techniques developed through this research will be implemented in the Mexican amaranth workshop associated with the Presidium.

The first batch of amaranth flour and seeds has already arrived at the University, and trials and analyses both of the baking qualities of the plant and greenhouse trials have begun. The results of this collaboration will be presented at the Salone del Gusto in 2006.

## The Presidium

The NGO Alternativas y Procesos de Participación Social (Alternatives and Projects for Civil Society), which has been working since 1980 to recover traditional knowledge of cultivation and irrigation systems, is now involved in recovering amaranth. Alternativas has organized cooperatives in sixty villages, involving 1,100 native families in the region of Mixteca. Each family now plants a maximum of a quarter of a hectare of amaranth, and in the rest of its plot of land (*milpa*) plants a mix of corn, beans, peppers and pumpkin. The cooperatives have come together to create a larger cooperative grouping capable of producing amaranth-based foodstuffs under a common brand name: in the Náhuatl language this name means 'good'.

The Presidium will work in three main areas: promoting a traditional sweet food based on amaranth (*alegría*); developing experimental amaranth-based products which can be used in gluten-free diets, with the long-term goal of increasing the amaranth market; and setting up a center for exhibiting, growing and selling amaranth in a 'Water Museum' which will also host other Mexican Presidia and thus become an important focal point where people can learn about biodiversity and pre-Hispanic traditions.

**Production Area**
Mexico
Puebla State
Tehuacán Valley

**Producers**
1100 families united in
*Alternativas y Procesos de Participación Social*

**Presidium Coordinator**
Raúl Hernandez Garciadiego
Tel. +52 238 3712550
raulhdezg@laneta.apc.org

# Andean Fruit

## Tomatillo, Poro Poro and Pushgay

The Cajamarca Region at the foot of the Andes boasts an extraordinary variety of domesticated plants, particularly tubers, grains, and fruit. Fruits from this region vary greatly in color and shape. This great range can be attributed to the wealth of this region's natural resources and also to the worldview of the pre-Columbian peoples of the region. According to the Incas, all forms of life—men, animals, vegetables, as well as wind, streams, and land—are intimately connected. Respect for this connection has certainly contributed to conservationism here.

From the numerous native species, the Presidium has selected three fruits that are popular fresh and preserved in jams: Tomatillo, Poro Poro, and Pushgay. The Tomatillo (*Physalis peruviana*) is also known as *aguaymanto*, *poha*, or *alkekengi*. This round berry owes its resemblance to a small Chinese lantern to the fine, papery husk that envelops the fruit. When ripe, it is bright yellow-orange in color and boasts a tangy sweetness which is perfect paired with savory dishes featuring fish, red meat, and particularly wild game. The Tomatillo is also used to make jam, ice-cream, liqueurs, and fermented beverages. The fruit is an excellent source of phosphorus and protein. Its extensive root system serves an important role in protecting hillsides from erosion.

The Poro Poro or *galupa* (*Passiflora pinnastipula*) is a climbing perennial with showy flowers and yellow, oblong fruits packed with small seeds. The flesh of the Poro Poro is like that of an orange, and the fruit has a strong, lingering perfume. Poro Poro is crushed to make refreshing beverages, jams, and sorbets and can also be used to dress salads.

Pushgay (*Vaccinium floribundum*), also known as *mortiño*, grows on wild bushes on the highest, rockiest peaks of Cajamarca and produces fruit similar to European blueberries: small dark blue berries that ripen to a deep blue-black. Pushgay berries are used to make jam, liqueurs, and sorbets and are an excellent accompaniment for lamb.

## The Presidium

Created in collaboration with the NGO ANPE (*Asociación nacional de Productores Ecológicos*), the Presidium has worked to identify the traditional region of production for the fruit varieties selected for the project and has assembled a group of eight producers interested in working together.

Currently, the production of Tomatillo and Poro Poro is limited to small family farms, and the Pushgay is collected from wild fruit trees at high altitude. The technique of producing Tomatillo and Poro Poro is sustainable and prohibits the use of fertilizers and pesticides.

The objective of the project is to define a protocol outlining both the cultivation of the fruit and the production of jams, juices, and other products based on the fruit. In the case of the Pushgay, the goal is to identify a variety of the plant that is suitable for selection and cultivation with a view to farming the fruit.

The project's more immediate aim is to unite the producers in an association that facilitates the involvement of local technicians and experts to improve the quality of products made from the fruit varieties. The next step is to promote these fruits and products locally, nationally, and internationally.

**Production Area**
Peru
Cajamarca Department
Cajamarca, San Marcos, Chota and
Baños del Inca Provinces

**Producers**
Eight farmers united in
ANPE (*Asociación Nacional de
Productores Ecológicos*)

**Presidium Coordinators**
Rubén Figueroa Llanos
Tel. +51 076823429
figruben@mixmail.com

Mario Tapia
Tel. +51 14757970
mariotapia@amauta.rcp.net.pe

# Andean Potatoes

## Peru's Nine Hundred Potato Varieties

Legend has it that when the first Inca, Manco Cápac, and his wife, Mama Ocllo, emerged from Lake Titicaca to build their empire, the great god Wircocha explained to him first thing how to plant corn in the lowlands and potatoes on the high plains. Originating from the central Peruvian and Bolivian Andes, potatoes are farmed across these mountains and symbolize the agriculture and gastronomy of the people who live there. While in Europe and North America primarily the *Solanum tuberosum* potato species is cultivated, in the Andes there are nine species of potatoes. Farmers have selected these species for color, shape, and flavor and have diversified them into 900 varieties.

Andean Potatoes are divided into bitter and non-bitter families, and the latter type are all called *dulce* in Spanish. *Dulce* potatoes have almost none of the toxic, bitter alkaloid solanin and therefore can be prepared as regular potatoes. The bitter potatoes, each with varying quantities of solanin, cannot be eaten raw but must be dried and reconstituted.

The Presidium is working to protect five specific varieties. The Locka and the Ococuri are bitter potatoes, grown in the freezing terraced beds of altitudes ranging from 3,800 to 4,200 meters above sea level. The Locka is slightly flattened and cream-colored while the Ococuri has a blue-violet or white skin. The other three varieties are *dulce*, and can be cultivated from 3,300 to 3,900 meters: the Ccompis, Pitiquiña, and Mactillo. The round Ccompis has deep eyes, rosy skin and white flesh, the Pitiquiña is long and oval with floury flesh, and the Mactillo has a violet peel and white flesh streaked with violet. Because bitter potatoes can be conserved for many years, they offer a very important and reliable food source. The most important preserved food made from bitter potatoes is *chuño blanco* or *negro*, which is also known as *tunta* or *morata*. To make *chuño*, potatoes are pulled from the ground, doused with water, and left outside for three consecutive nights in the freezing months of May and June. Then the frozen potatoes are placed in cloth bags or straw baskets and stored in running water for three weeks. The potatoes are then pulled from the water and left for another night in the freezing open air, beaten to a pulp and left to dry. The dried *chuño* can be reconstituted quickly with water to make a simple meal. The smaller bitter potatoes are simply peeled, cut into small pieces, and dried in the sun.

## The Presidium

This Presidium is carried out in partnership with the Peruvian organic association ANPE (Asociación nacional de Productores Ecológicos). In the project's first phase, the Presidium has selected the five most interesting varieties from an agricultural and gastronomic perspective and has begun work with eight farmers, who will improve the quality of the seed stock and dedicate more land to growing potatoes for seed potato selection.

The next objective is to define a production protocol for each variety that guarantees the traceability of the potatoes, prohibits the use of pesticides and fertilizers, and ensures the quality of the final product.

The selection and production of seed potatoes will allow the Presidium to increase production and the number of producers involved in upcoming years. In a second phase, the Presidium will develop products based on the potato varieties for sale to a wider market.

**Production Area**
Peru
Calca Province - Cusco Region
Municipality of Lares
Melgar Province - Puno Region
Municipalities of Keska, Umasullo, and Ayaviri

**Producers**
Eight farmers united in the *Asociación Nacional de Productores Ecológicos*

**Presidium Coordinator**
Edgardo Cáceres and Moisés Quispe
Tel. +511 4235756
caceresparraguez@yahoo.com

Mario Tapia
Tel. +511 4757970
mariotapia@amauta.rcp.net.pe

**Presidium supported by**
Saclà

# American Raw Milk Cheeses

### Fighting for Raw Milk Rights

The first American cheeses were modeled on English and Dutch products and later on German and Italian ones, as immigrants brought their cheesemaking skills and traditions to the New World. Over the past 200 years, American cheesemakers have 'domesticated' these cheeses by making versions of traditional European cheeses. Dry Jack, Teleme, and Brick are examples of American cheeses based on European originals (Parmesan, Taleggio, and Limberger, respectively). In the past few decades, new American cheesemakers, many of them women, have created a wide spectrum of innovative artisan cheeses.

Often invented or based loosely on existing cheeses, these products are as unique as the cheesemakers themselves and they reflect as much persona as they do *terroir*. Hard, soft, cooked curd, washed rind, pressed, wrapped, they vary from huge 40 kilo wheels to tiny 100 gram forms, and are wrapped in leaves, sprinkled with ash, or crusted in salt. The cheeses included in Slow Food's first American Presidium project have a few common denominators: the use of raw milk from either the cheesemaker's or a local farm, and a powerful commitment to sustainable agriculture and artisan production. Many of these cheesemakers are 'farmstead' producers, using only the milk from their herd. Promoting farmstead means limiting the size of the farms involved (usually small family concerns) and adding an extra guarantee of quality.

The smallholders who make these artisan cheeses are usually working singly or only with their families. They make cheese daily and sell the vast majority at a weekly farmers' markets or directly to local restaurants, not through distribution networks. Given that they are selling at a tiny farmers' market where they might be the only cheese seller on hand, they may need to produce up to 10 or 12 different types of cheese—with one herd of 25 cows—to satisfy all the local needs: fresh cheese, grating cheese, cooking cheese, and table cheese. It's difficult to focus on any single variety when producing such a range of products, but it is the only way for a small producer to survive.

## The Presidium

In the United States, the sale of raw milk cheeses that are aged less than 60 days is illegal, and cheesemakers are also at risk of losing the right to produce all raw milk cheese altogether. Due to the lack of a regional identity and the difficulties in collaboration between different producers (they may be hundreds of miles apart), the situation facing American raw milk cheese producers is challenging. Small cheesemakers feel isolated and, in addition to the problems involved in running a business, have to contend with the problems of uncertain and ever-changing health and food safety regulations. To put the project on a firm base, Slow Food has had to reconsider the normal structure of a Presidium and focus on the objectives. The result is a project involving over 30 producers, connected not by historical or geographic links but by common aims: the improvement of quality of American raw milk cheeses and the creation of links between cheesemakers. A group of tasters, comprising Slow Food and cheesemaking experts, select the best raw milk farmstead cheeses each year from among participating producers. These cheeses will become the ambassadors of the project, representing the Presidium in different events and serving as an example of high quality for American producers. The Presidium has organized educational exchanges for cheesemakers, as well as tastings and promotional events.

| Production Area | Producers | Presidium Coordinator |
|---|---|---|
| United States | Thirty cheesemakers | Robert La Valva |
| | | Slow Food USA |
| | | Tel. +1 718 260 8000 |
| | | rlavalva@earthlink.net |

# Anishinaabeg Manoomin

### The Good Grain

In the month of September, the indigenous North American Anishinaabeg people (also known as Ojibwe) begin the rice harvest; they call the month the 'wild rice moon.' Each day, the harvesters head out in canoes to harvest wild rice from the smooth surface of lakes with names like Blackbird, Big, Pigeon, and, naturally, Rice Lake. They harvest the rice in pairs, often husband and wife, with the 'poler' sitting towards the front pushing the boat through the stands of rice, and the 'knocker' sitting towards the rear, hitting the rice stalks with a pole and knocking the grains into the canoe—a pair of good 'ricers' can harvest two hundred and fifty kilos on a good day.

The Ojibwe people call wild rice Manoomin, which means 'the good grain'. It was so easy to cultivate that the Anishinaabeg thought of it as a 'savior' grain—it grew naturally, with no need to be planted or tended, and provided a bountiful harvest that could be put away for the whole winter. The existence of wild rice in the Americas predates Minnesota's first indigenous population by at least a millennium, and given that it has never been selected for specific traits, the wild rice growing in the state today has probably changed little from that of prehistory.

In Anishinaabeg lore, wild rice was a gift: a hunter named Nanaboozhoo discovered the grain when he came home one night with nothing to eat. According to the folk tale,

## The Presidium

The wild rice promoted by the Presidium is harvested in the remote lakes of northern Minnesota of the White Earth Reservation, inhabited by the Anishinaabeg tribe. But 95% of what is sold as wild rice today in the United States is actually grown in paddies, primarily in California, although it is still called 'wild.' Another threat facing this traditional indigenous North American product is destruction of the natural ecosystems of the Minnesota lakes through recreational zoning of the lakes, damming, and agricultural runoff.

The Presidium will work with the existing project developed by Native Harvest as part of the White Earth Land Recovery Project to promote consumption of traditionally harvested and prepared wild rice.

'There was a duck sitting on the edge of his kettle of boiling water. After the duck flew away, Nanaboozhoo looked into the kettle and found wild rice floating upon the water, it was the best soup he had ever tasted. Later, he followed the direction the duck had taken and came upon a lake of manoomin.' Another tale from tribal lore says that the Anishinaabeg once lived in the East and moved after a visionary told them to walk west until they found the place where food grew upon the water.

Wild rice is an aquatic grass and is not actually part of the rice family at all. Japonica and Indica rice are part of the *Oryza* genera, while Manoomin's genera is *Zizania*—genetically, it is more similar to corn than rice. Unlike regular rice, it cannot be simply dried and eaten. The fresh grains of rice—all colors of green, tan, and brown—are husked and then parched in a wide shallow drum. The parching highlights wild rice's naturally toasted flavor.

Manoomin tastes richly complex with notes of mushrooms, forest undergrowth, and wood smoke. As a whole grain, it must be cooked carefully to prevent the grains from splitting and to retain the crispy full texture of the rice.

| Production Area | Producers | Presidium Coordinators | Presidium supported by |
|---|---|---|---|
| United States<br>Minnesota State<br>Anishinaabeg tribal lands | 200 gatherers | Winona La Duke and Sarah Alexander<br>White Earth Land Recovery Project<br>Tel. +1 218 573 3049-218 234 1951<br>salexander@welrp.org | Consorzio Tutela Vini<br>Oltrepò Pavese |

# Cape May
# Salt Oyster

### From the Delaware Bay Oyster Flats

The town of Cape May was once filled with large heaps of shells bleached white by the sun and its port was lined with long buildings facing the water. Oysters once streamed out of here: they were collected in barrels, loaded onto trucks and dispatched to Philadelphia. The shells are all that remain of the past glory of Delaware Bay, sheltered by the slender peninsula ending at Cape May, where Delaware, New Jersey and Pennsylvania meet.

In Colonial Philadelphia the sellers used to clatter up and down the streets, which were often paved with shells; the oysters were eaten raw, in stew, preserved in brine or fried and served with chicken salad. Back then, places selling oysters were as common as present-day pizzerias.

Overfishing, pollution, increased water temperatures and parasitic diseases are responsible for the crisis which began during the Great Depression and saw oysters decrease in both number and size. While the estuary was home to 1,400 boats with 2,300 men in 1879, there are now fewer than 50 boats and 150 men involved in cultivating and gathering oysters. Some studies maintain that the oyster farms in the upper bay were already destroyed during the Second World War due to sailing boats being replaced by motor boats. But today the bay is cleaner, partly due to environmental programs implemented by the three states and partly due to the decline of heavy industry in Philadelphia. These reasons encourage optimism that local oysters can once again flourish in their habitat.

## Oysters in the Gold Fields

"In remote and seldom-visited valleys of the Sierras, I have grown solemn over the supposition that mine were the first footsteps which had ever indented the soil. And then I have turned but to behold the gaping, ripped cylinders scattered like dew over the land, and labeled 'Oysters'." Prentice Mulford, *Overland Monthly*, 1869

The rush to conquer the American West in the 1850s was no high point in the history of American cuisine. The men who went out to California to make their fortunes in the gold mines came from France, Argentina, and Italy, as well as America's eastern seaboard and southern states, but when they got to the Sierra Nevada they ate the local crude fare of bacon, beans, and sourdough bread. As the mines grew, gold came pouring into the pockets of these isolated tribes of mountain men, and they began to seek food that represented their new wealth. One mania was fresh eggs, another fine French wine, while the third and longest-lasting fad in the gold camps were canned oysters—all paid for with gold dust, naturally. Oysters then as now represented luxury, and the invention of a canning process for oysters coincided with a heyday in the California camps. Across the country in Delaware Bay (among other East Coast oyster grounds), thousands of oysters were loaded onto trains to Philadelphia, from there to Boston, and then on around the horn to San Francisco. By the 1870s, Cape May had a railway that extended right down to the docks, where the oysters were shucked, packed into barrels, and shipped off for canning. Production peaked quickly, however, when locals found oyster beds along the San Francisco coast and fresh oysters became easily available. But the fad launched the Delaware Bay beds, and contributed to the over-fishing which had sapped the bay's stocks by the turn of the century.

## The Presidium

The Cape May Salt Oyster has become a Slow Food Presidium to maintain a low environmental-impact system of cultivation tried and tested in France. According to this technique, oyster sprats are produced in hatcheries and then placed on nets hanging from racks stretching across the shallows exposed to the tide. These oysters, 'planted' in the sea, feed naturally by filtering ocean water and are not given any artificial feed or antibiotics. The success of these new sustainable farms is a sign of the bay's recovered health, which Slow Food wishes to promote by supporting the activity of the few remaining fishermen and significantly developing the local and international market for oysters. A first promotional initiative has already been accomplished with the Hotel Plaza in New York serving raw Cape May oysters on large trays of ice in its Oyster Bar.

**Production Area**
United States
New Jersey State
Delaware Bay
Cape May

**Producers**
Five aquaculturists, only one of whom distributes commercially

**Presidium Coordinators**
Jim Weaver
Slow Food Convivium Leader
Tel. +1 609 452 1515
jim@trepiani.com

Hans-Jakob Werlen
Slow Food Convivium Leader
Tel. +1 610 328 8612
hwerlen1@swarthmore.edu

# Heritage Turkey Breeds

**Truly American Birds**   When Benjamin Franklin wrote to his daughter in 1784 to weigh in with his thoughts on what animal best symbolized the United States, he described the turkey as the perfect emblem: 'Eagles have been found in all Countries, but the Turkey is peculiar to ours'.

Turkeys are native to the Americas and were a primary source of meat for many Native American tribes, but the domesticated varieties we know today originated in Europe. Collectors brought back these birds from the New World in the sixteenth century to breed and select for their meat- and egg-producing capabilities in Britain, Holland, France, and Germany. American settlers then brought back the domesticated turkeys and the progeny of native wild birds and European varieties gave rise to American domestic breeds. Prior to the industrialization of turkey production, which began at the turn of the century, nearly every family farm in the United States kept a small flock of these fowl. The birds grazed freely, ate varied diets, roosted in trees and grew to full size in seven or more months.

The turkeys eaten in America today are not the splendid half-wild birds that Benjamin Franklin thought so noble. Nearly all of the 270 million turkeys raised now are the one variety known as the Large White that was introduced in the 1950s and was subsequently bred to meet the needs of industrial production. While Large Whites grow very rapidly (reaching maturity in just two months), they are unable to mate naturally and are typically fed a diet high in fat and dosed with antibiotics.

The eight varieties of Heritage Turkeys are known as sub-breeds, the primary distinctions among them being their colors and the region where they were first selected. 'Heritage' is a general name that refers to the family of historic American turkey sub-breeds: Standard Bronze, Narragansett, Bourbon Red, Jersey Buff, Slate, White Holland, Beltsville Small White, and Royal Palm.

When Heritage Turkeys are raised free-range on pasture and forage, they develop much stronger legs, thighs, and breasts than industrially-produced turkeys, which have mostly breast meat. The resulting meat from these Heritage birds is very firm and dark in color, as well as being succulent, rich and flavorful. These turkeys are excellent roasted whole or

## Turkey Day

On the third Thursday of November, American families gather at the table to commemorate the first harvest of the Plymouth colony in 1621, which ensured their survival after a winter of great suffering and near starvation. The seventeenth-century colonists and Native Americans feasted on venison, wild fowl, lobster, boiled vegetables and stewed fruits on Thanksgiving Day, but today, the meal varies according to region. Yankees from the Northeast lay their tables with platters of red flannel hash, cream biscuits, and cranberry-apple relish. In the New England states, a terrain of potatoes, apples, and root vegetables, the local produce is also employed in breads thickened with potato starch, turnip and rutabaga casseroles, creamed onions, and apple pie wrapped in a lard crust. In the South, deep orange sweet potatoes are covered with a browned crust of marshmallows and dried corn is cooked in heavy cream, in succotash or spoonbread. Midwestern Thanksgivings reflect the region's Swedish and German heritage, with savory casseroles dense with pumpkin and turnips, and pickled beets. One common ingredient links Thanksgiving across the country: a roasted turkey at the center of the table. It is usually cooked slowly the entire morning of Thanksgiving and stuffed with bread seasoned with oysters, apples, chestnuts or sausage. The symbolism of the mahogany-brown roasted bird for Americans cannot be underestimated—it could never, say, be substituted by a leg of lamb. The market for turkeys is extremely seasonal (95% are sold in November), and the strength of this Presidium lies in its link to one of the strongest American food traditions.

## The Presidium

In 2001, Slow Food USA initiated a Presidium to reintroduce Heritage Turkeys to American consumers. The initial goal of the Presidium has been to encourage farmers to raise the eight traditional varieties, as most of them remain perilously close to extinction. Results of this effort have been encouraging: in 2001, Slow Food's partner on this project, the American Livestock Breeds Conservancy (ALBC), estimated that fewer than 1,200 breeding turkeys of all eight Heritage varieties remained in the entire country. By 2004, the population of breeding birds had increased to 4,000. Slow Food is now working with the ALBC and with turkey farmers to develop protocol for the Presidium that will outline sustainable and humane production of Heritage Turkeys with high taste quality.

| Production Area | Producers | Presidium Coordinator |
|---|---|---|
| United States | 30 farms | Robert La Valva<br>Slow Food USA<br>Tel. +1 212 677 9695<br>rlavalva@earthlink.net |

# Asia

| 1 | China | Tibetan Plateau Yak Cheese |
| 2 | India | Dehradun Basmati |
| 3 | India | Mustard Seed Oil |
| 4 | Malaysia | Bario Rice |

# Tibetan Plateau Yak Cheese

94

## The Nomadic Shepherds of Golok

The Golok Prefecture is at the center of the Qinghai-Tibetan plateau, an enormous oval plain with such long, level stretches of land that the nomads' thick yak-wool tents can be seen from miles away.

At this altitude of 4,500 meters, the lush green expanses of meadows are broken by hundreds of hardy low-flowering plants and by the tall, arched backs of grazing black and white yaks. Eagles are a regular sight overhead, and flocks of goats and sheep also feed on the high plains grass.

The yaks graze the pastures in the plains surrounding Maqin County in Golok and in the high, deep valleys that extend from the plain like spokes. The milk of the female yak, the *dri*, is often drunk fresh and is also made into yogurt that can be eaten fresh. First boiled, then pressed, the whey can also be used to make a hard cheese that is laid out in the sun to dry. The most important product made from the milk is butter, which is eaten fresh but can also be aged for up to a year. The traditional breakfast of the Golok herdsmen consists of a little *tsampa*, or toasted barley, mixed with whole yak milk and a few tablespoons of yak butter, all warmed together to make a rough porridge.

At a small dairy located about an hour's drive from the noted Ragya monastery in a magnificent valley near Golok, Tibetan and Nepalese cheesemakers make a range of Tibetan and European-style cheeses from yak milk that

arrives in the dairy just a few hours after milking.

At the Ragya dairy, copper cheese-making vats are heated by burning thick pads of dry yak manure. The cheese is made twice daily: the first shift lasts from eight in the morning until one in the afternoon, and the second from eight in the evening until one or two in the morning. The cheeses made in these extreme conditions showcase the excellent pasture of the region. Yaks yield low quantities of dense, rich milk which can be as much as 7% fat. This milk is skimmed for cheesemaking and retains a splendid flavor similar to that of springtime sheep milk. The cheese can taste like a rough pecorino, and the aged forms develop strong grassy scents tempered by the milk's natural richness.

## The Presidium

This project is the fruit of a collaboration between the Trace Foundation, dedicated to promoting the cultural continuity and sustainable development of Tibetan communities within China, and Slow Food. The Trace Foundation has invested in building a cheesemaking plant on the Qinghai-Tibetan Plateau, and Slow Food has recently become involved in the project with the goal of developing a cheese based on Tibetan yak milk that is both innovative and traditional.

Traditionally, local yak milk products include the aforementioned yogurt, butter, and hard cheese, designed with long nomadic hikes in mind. Fresh products like yogurt and butter cannot be distributed easily, as the nearest market is a six-hour drive away. The cheeses are so spicy and hard that they are difficult to sell outside the region of origin. To produce a cheese that showcases the excellent quality of the pasture-fed yak milk and to provide a viable income for the region's nomadic herders, the only possible solution was to develop a European-style cheese that could be aged and therefore transported easily.

At the same time, a Presidium must also maintain strong links to the local territory, and therefore this innovative product had to include aspects of local culture, such as the strong link with nomadic life and the abundance of the region's pasture.

To answer this challenge, Slow Food sent Ernst Holenstein and Andrea Adami, Swiss and Italian cheesemakers, respectively, and Massimo Mercandino, an Italian technician from the Veterinary Association for Cooperation in Developing Countries (AVEC).

After three months of experimentation, the team developed a Swiss-style hard cheese made of partially-skimmed milk that is well-suited to yak milk.

This Presidium is still in its initial phase, and in upcoming years the experimentation will continue. The current challenges include the exportation of the product and the development of the local market.

**Production Area**
China
Maqin County
Golok Prefecture
Qinghai Province

**Producers**
35 nomadic shepherds and five
cheesemakers who work in the Ragya
dairy

**Technical Partner**
AVEC - Veterinary Association for
Cooperation in Developing Countries

**Presidium Coordinator**
Paola Vanzo
pVanzo@trace.org

**Presidium supported by**
Trace Foundation

# Dehradun
## Basmati Rice

### Fragrant Grains
### from the Himalayas

Basmati rice varieties were developed over centuries in the agricultural lands carved out of the foothills of the Himalayas. The first written reference to Basmati rice dates back to the beginning of the eighteenth century, and since then, farmers have developed hundreds of types of this fragrant variety.

Today, Basmati paddies can be found around the world, but it is in the Indian Himalayas near the area where the rice variety was first developed that some of the best Basmati rice is still grown. Dehradun Basmati is cultivated in the State of Uttar Pradesh near the town of Dehradun in the foothills of the Himalayas and in the State of Uttaranchal, high in the Himalayan range. On the hillsides where Dehradun Basmati is cultivated, terraces are cut into the mountain slopes, surrounded by supporting walls made of clay, mud and weeds with openings for water outflow and inflow. The tools used for rice production here are simple: sickles, wooden ploughs, and bullock carts. The past use of pesticides in these remote Himalayan valleys has caused environmental damage and contributed to the emergence of chemical-resistant pests. In response to these problems, Dehradun Basmati rice is cultivated without pesticides. There are various plants traditionally used for pest control in the paddies, as well as natural anti-parasitic substances such as ash and cow urine.

Basmati rice can range in color from clear yellow to deep dark brown, with scents as diverse as jasmine and sandalwood. In Dehradun cuisine, Basmati is prized for its fragrance and dishes using the local rice accent this special scent. For example, *khichdi*, a local dish for festivities, is made of Basmati and mung beans seasoned with cardamom, *garam masala* and spiked with cashew nuts. *Khichdi* is traditionally served at the harvest festival Sankranti, where the combination of rice and pulses symbolizes plenty and prosperity. *Kheer*, a sweet milky rice pudding, is a very auspicious dish, made in Dehradun during all festive occasions as an offering to the gods and guests. Kheer prepared with Basmati is very creamy and is seasoned with cardamom, slivers of almonds, and raisins. When preparing these and other dishes from Dehradun Basmati, it is common to add a few cloves to the boiling water of the rice steamer to heighten flavor and aroma.

## The Presidium

The Dehradun Basmati Presidium has been developed with the Navdanya Trust, which was created by Vandana Shiva to conserve indigenous seed varieties, protect traditional food cultures, and fight agricultural patents. Navdanya, which means 'nine seeds' in Hindi, works with more than 60,000 farmers to promote seed banks throughout Northern India and to develop organic agriculture in India.

This Presidium promotes a number of Basmati varieties, selected for their flavor and aroma: the Punjab Basmati, wonderfully fragrant with long, clear yellow grains; Dehradun Desi Basmati, rich with floral scents and notes of sandalwood; and Kasturi Basmati, redolent of mint and lemon.

The Presidium is working to promote Dehradun Basmati rice varieties both nationally and internationally through events, publications, and dinners. Currently, 80 producers have been confirmed as part of the project by adhering to the Presidium production protocol standards, and the aim is to add 40 new producers per year.

**Production Area**
India
Uttar Pradesh State, Saharanpur
(Punjab Basmati, Desi Basmati)
Uttaranchal State
(Kasturi Basmati, Dehradun)

**Producers**
80 farmers that work with the Navdanya Research Foundation

**Technical Partner**
Risi & Co-Gli Aironi (Italy)

**Presidium Coordinator**
Maya Jani
Navdanya Seed Conservation Movement
Tel. +91 11 6561868
navdanya_ad@hotmail.com
www.navdanya.org

**Presidium supported by**
Planeta

# Mustard Seed Oil

## India's Spicy Oil

India is one of the world's primary producers of oil seeds. Mustard, in particular, is cultivated throughout India, and is especially characteristic of the states of Rajasthan, Uttar Pradesh, West Bengal, Bihar, Jammu, Kashmir, Haryana, Himachal Pradesh, Madhya Pradesh and Gujarat. In these regions, mustard oil is used in almost every dish to enrich flavor with its spiciness.

Small producers plant mustard because it guarantees a high yield with low production costs. The work of mustard cultivation is divided by gender: men work in the fields and tend the plants, while women plant the mustard and harvest the seeds and leaves. The harvested seeds are pressed in *ghani*, or small mills.

Mustard is a symbol of springtime and rebirth and plays a fundamental role in Indian culture. The seeds and oil are important in the rite of Hindu marriage, and in April, when the plants blossom with yellow flowers, it is traditional to dress in the colors of mustard for the springtime festival of Basant.

Mustard leaves, seeds, and oil are all crucial to Indian cuisine. Dishes like Punjab corn bread with mustard leaves (*Makki ki roti* with *Sarson ka Saag*) feature the fresh green leaves of the plant. Countless Indian specialties are built upon the spicy flavor of mustard oil. Hilsa fish, fried in mustard oil, is a specialty of the Bengal region. Northern Indians adore *pakoras* (battered vegetables fried in mustard oil), while in the South of India, dried mustard seed is used as a spice.

Mustard seed oil is also important to traditional Ayurvedic medicine, where it is used for massages and to cure muscular pains. Mustard has antimycotic properties and helps cure dermatological diseases.

During winter, the oil is used to condition dry hair and is also considered a preventative medicine against arthritis. The oil is also burned in *diya*, the traditional lamp that is the symbol of Deepawali, the festival of the lights. During the festival, the smoke from the burning *diya* cleans the air of houses, driving away impurities and bad air.

## The Presidium

This Presidium has been created with the support and advice of Vandana Shiva of the Navdana Seed Conservation Movement. The project involves farming families from the village of Chanadn Hari in Utter Pradesh. The primary objective of the Presidium is to improve the collection, selection, conservation and distribution of various mustard varieties. A second goal is conversion to organic agriculture. Through this collaboration between Slow Food and Navdanya, the Presidium hopes to create a local cooperative that will connect producers to consumers through local markets modelled on farmers' markets.

The Presidium has been set up with the assistance of Slow Food Tuscany, particularly Slow Food Valdarno, and with the support of the Provincial Authority and Chamber of Commerce of Arezzo.

**Production Area**
India
Uttar Pradesh State
Chanadn Hari village

**Producers**
25 families

**Presidium Coordinator**
Maya Jani and Birendra Chhetri
Navdanya Seed Conservation
Movement
Tel. +91 11 26561868
navdanya_ad@hotmail.com
www.navdanya.org

**Presidium supported by**
Province of Arezzo

# Bario Rice

## Sowing Rice in Sarawak

The Bario Rice variety originated in the remote highlands of the same name at an average altitude of around 1,100 meters in the north-east of the Malaysian state of Sarawak, on the island of Borneo. Twenty years ago, this region could be reached only after a week of hard walking. Today, a small biplane flies there daily, but the preferred means of transit remains the buffalo. Bario Rice is native to these high plains and is cultivated manually by the local Kelabit tribe. Bario's yield per hectare is very low compared to hybrid varieties, amounting to two and three tons per hectare compared to the ten tons produced by commercial hybrids.

The terrain here has been transformed into rice paddies through centuries of labor. Paddies have been sculpted from the mountainside, creating narrow fields with just enough space for a buffalo to turn around as it tills. The Kelabit tribe has brought water to even the most remote fields with an intricate system of bamboo tubes. With the introduction of modern, high-yield varieties in Sarawak, the older rice varieties are slowly losing ground. Most rice farmers in Sarawak still follow the traditional planting technique of mixing a number of different varieties in order to stagger the harvest period and to reduce the risk of crop failure; some farmers plant as many as eight varieties in just a hectare or two, but most plant about three or four.

In Sarawak, each family cultivates an area of one to two hectares of rice. Terraced hillside fields are preferred by the majority of the rural population, and the traditional farming system practiced here is 'shifting cultivation', with a short but variable cultivation alternating with a long, equally variable fallow period.

In Bario, farmers treat the planting of rice with great reverence, celebrating the occasion with various rituals and ceremonies. The *Bumai piring* celebration commemorates the preparation of the land and *piring ngepong padi* inaugurates the harvest. During the growing season, certain rituals protect the crop from evil spirits and omens.

The farmers prepare and sow the fields in July and then harvest the rice in January. Buffalo live on the fallow fields, eating the weeds and fertilizing the soil.

Bario rice has tiny, very white opaque grains. Famous in Sarawak, it is a favorite among Malaysian chefs, who appreciate its gummy quality. It adapts well to traditional preparations like *lemang*, in which the rice is cooked while tightly packed in banana leaves and steamed in a cane of bamboo, allowing it to form a single dense mass. Bario rice is ideal for desserts like rice pudding and rice pie, where its fine consistency and light perfume give delicate results.

## Have you eaten rice today?

In longhouses in the highlands of Sarawak, a common greeting is '*Mbuh maan tubi andu ati,*' or, 'Have you eaten rice today?'. Rice is eaten all day long here, starting first thing in the morning with a breakfast of steamed glutinous rice fermented with yeast and wrapped in coconut leaves. For lunch, farmers take plain cooked rice wrapped in simpoh leaves (*sukui*) to the fields with them. At dinnertime, rice is cooked in oil with meat (*pandang*), steamed in bamboo tubes (*pogang*), cooked in bamboo mixed with coconut milk and wrapped in banana leaves (*lemang*), and made into porridge (*tube jariek*).

Rice is always included in the offerings made to the gods for family celebrations like naming a child, a funeral, or a wedding. On these occasions, the gods are offered popped rice (*retup*), rice cooked in coconut leaves (*ketupat*), glutinous rice in bamboo (*pulut dalam buloh*) and rice cake (*pengana*). These snacks are accompanied by *tuak*, a wine made from glutinous or waxy rice, and *langkau*, an alcohol distilled from *tuak*.

## The Presidium

Bario Rice is an important example of agricultural biodiversity. It is a local product cultivated with no pesticides or herbicides by the Kelabit tribe whose members, numbering fewer than 5,000 people, live exclusively in the highlands.

The Presidium has been developed to give concrete assistance to local growers and thus help them reach a more remunerative market. In the long term, the Presidium will work to develop seed farms that will aid the conservation of diverse strains of Bario rice and perpetuate the purest versions of this extraordinary variety.

---

**Production Area**
Malaysia
Island of Borneo
Sarawak State
Kelabit high plains

**Producers**
150 ethnic Kelabit families

**Technical Partner**
Risi & Co-Gli Aironi (Italy)

**Presidium Coordinator**
Gien Kheng Teo
Tel. +60 82 611171
tfanfare@tm.net.my

# The World in a Grain of Rice

### The Vital Grain

In the Vietnamese, Japanese, Laotian and Thai languages the verb 'to eat' can be translated as 'to eat rice'. Rice means 'food' literally and tangibly. Rice fields occupy 10% of the world's farmland. In some countries like Cambodia, rice provides 80% of daily calories, while in Burma, per capita annual consumption is 211 kilos.

In these countries, rice is the main course, side dish, dessert, wine, beer, and after-dinner tipple. It has been grown for eight millennia and has shaped farmlands, economies, governments and societies.

No other crop has adapted so well to different landscapes: it survives below sea-level and at altitudes of 3,000 meters; on the equator and in the cold Hungarian steppes; in Manchuria and in the freezing Japanese island of Hokkaido; in areas with more than five meters of rain per year and others with barely ten centimeters.

It is no coincidence that a genetically modified rice variety was chosen to represent the good faith of genetic engineering in agriculture. Dubbed 'Golden Rice', this vitamin A-enriched crop was vaunted by agricultural multinationals as evidence of good intentions and of its capacity to address world hunger.

## The Taste of Rice

To taste and to cook rice, you have to keep the characteristics of the two primary rice varieties in mind.

The sensory differences between the two large families of rice, Indica and Japonica, are notable. A white 'pearl' can almost always be seen at the heart of the Japonica grain, and is usually absent in the Indica. This milky area is visible at the grain's center (or on the edge, in which case it is called a stripe) and indicates that the starch cells in the rice are not completely sealed. This pearl means there are tiny air pockets inside the grains, which are emptied of air when heated and fill up with water or fat. Water in the grains is to be avoided when making risotto or paella, so the rice is first toasted: it is poured onto the bubbling fat and browned a little before adding water or broth. The larger the grains and their pearl, the longer the browning takes (Arborio rice takes longer than Carnaroli, for example). This process ensures that the air pocket is filled with fat and the surface is sealed at the same time, so that liquid will not penetrate during cooking. The second element distinguishing Japonica and Indica is the percentage of amylose and amylopectin starches, which are the starches contained in rice. In the Japonica variety the quantity of amylopectin is much higher, and its molecular structure allows easier penetration of aromas and cooking liquid. Indica varieties, on the other hand, have a higher content of amylose which keeps the grain firm after cooking.

This is why only Japonica varieties are used for risotto while Indica is more suitable for dishes requiring boiled rice.

## 150,000 Different Grains

Where do the 150,000 plus varieties of rice grown around the world come from?

The rice genus *Oryza* is divided into two main species: *Oryza sativa*, which is found all over the world, and *Oryza glaberrima*, red rice from the Niger delta that is grown in increasingly smaller quantities in West Africa. When we talk about rice, we are usually referring to *Oryza sativa*. The two principal varieties of *Oryza sativa* found on all the continents stem from this species: Indica and Japonica. The Himalayas cleanly divide the two rice cultures. Indica comes from the south, from the Malaysian peninsula to east Asia while Japonica developed to the north of the Himalayas, spreading through Europe. Indica has longer, clear and vitreous grains which do not absorb cooking liquid but remain firm. The Japonica varieties are completely different: the grains are shorter and absorb dressings and can easily be creamed into a paste. The main Italian rice varieties are Japonicas (Carnaroli, Arborio, Vialone Nano, Baldo...) as is the main Spanish variety, Bomba, which is the principal ingredient of paella. The large Indica family includes glutinous and aromatic rices. The aromatic varieties—basmati from India and Pakistan and jasmine from Thailand—have an aroma so strong it permeates the paddy fields.

# Europe

| | | |
|---|---|---|
| 1 | Bosnia-Herzegovina | Pozegaca Plum Slatko |
| 2 | Croatia | Giant Istrian Ox |
| 3 | Denmark | Artisan Salted Butter |
| 4 | France | Gascony Black Pig |
| 5 | France | Pardailhan Black Turnip |
| 6 | France | Rennes Coucou Chicken |
| 7 | France | Roussillon Dry Rancios Wine |
| 8 | France | Saint-Flour Planèze Golden Lentil |
| 9 | Greece | Mavrotragano |
| 10 | Greece | Niotiko |
| 11 | Hungary | Mangalica Sausage |
| 12 | Ireland | Irish Raw Cow Milk Cheese |
| 13 | Ireland | Irish Wild Smoked Salmon |
| 14 | The Netherlands | Aged Artisan Gouda |
| 15 | The Netherlands | Eastern Scheldt Lobster |
| 16 | The Netherlands | Texel Sheep Cheese |
| 17 | Poland | Oscypek |
| 18 | Poland | Polish Mead |
| 19 | Poland | Polish Red Cow |
| 20 | Portugal | Mirandesa Sausage |
| 21 | Spain | Euskal Txerria Pig |
| 22 | Spain | Gamonedo |
| 23 | Spain | Jiloca Saffron |
| 24 | Spain | Tolosa Black Beans |
| 25 | Sweden | Reindeer Suovas |
| 26 | Switzerland | Zincarlin |
| 27 | United Kingdom | Artisan Somerset Cheddar |
| 28 | United Kingdom | Cornish Salt Pilchard |
| 29 | United Kingdom | Gloucester Cheese |
| 30 | United Kingdom | Old Gloucester Beef |
| 31 | United Kingdom | Three Counties Perry |

● There are 198 Italian Presidia

# Bosnia-Herzegovina
# Pozegaca
# Plum Slatko

### Fruit From the Bosnian Borderland

Slatko, which means 'sweet' in Serbo-Croatian, is also the name for a preserve made of sweet, firm plums packed in dense sugar syrup made throughout Bosnia, Serbia, and Croatia. In the Upper Drina Valley near the city of Goradze in Bosnia-Herzegovina, the local interpretation of Slatko is particularly labor-intensive. First, the plums are doused with boiling water and then their skins are slipped off. Next, the pits are removed using a needle or skewer. The pitted and peeled plums are placed in water infused with lime for ten minutes to firm up their flesh and are then boiled in sugar syrup flavored with lemon slices. The conserve may also be flavored with cloves, walnuts or unpitted or halved plums, according to the maker's recipe.

The city of Goradze, about 120 kilometers southeast of Sarajevo, straddles the Drina River and is the heart of a Muslim enclave surrounded by a low horseshoe-shaped mountain range that touches the border of Serbia. This region's physical and cultural isolation made it a choice spot for weapons and chemical production for the united Yugoslavia. With the end of Communism, the bottom fell out of these industries, and unemployment soon soared to over 70%. The region was one of the hardest hit in the civil war when the valley endured a three-year siege.

Before communism, the Upper Drina was a fruit-producing area, and now, in the aftermath of the war, its residents are returning to orchards that were abandoned fifty years ago. While Slatko was once produced only in private homes and consumed for special occasions, local women are now producing it for income

Currently five women produce Presidium Slatko, but the group will expand with the success of the project. They have worked with several older women in Goradze to find the most traditional recipe, and their Slatko is cooked over a wooden fire in a village near Goradze with Pozegaca plums grown along the banks of the Drina River. The producers will form a cooperative this year with the assistance of the Italian NGO CEFA (European Committee for Agricultural Development), which is actively maintaining a large fruit nursery in the area. The producers are looking to commercialize their product locally in Goradze and Sarajevo, although they are collaborating with the Agropodrinje Cooperative, the project's Technical Partner, to ship internationally.

and employment. Pozegaca plums are used for Slatko in Goradze. This semi-wild local variety is never grafted but grown from seed—an unusual practice, as plum trees rarely grow 'true' from seed; they usually need to be grafted to produce identical fruits. It is possible that the Pozegaca variety has been isolated for so long in this valley that there is very little diversity. Given this stability, the Pozegaca, also known as the Franco-Slavo variety, is used for grafting many of the eating plums grown throughout Europe.

In the Upper Drina Valley, the first crop of Pozegaca plums, harvested throughout August, is eaten out of hand, while the second crop, harvested towards mid-September, is used for making Slatko and Slivovitz throughout the season. When picking the plums for Slatko, the women of Goradze look for fully ripe fruits that are small and have slightly shriveled skin at the stem end, which makes them easier to peel.

Once preserved, the plums have a wonderful light, creamy texture and a sweet flavor reminiscent of Turkish rose jam that pairs well with young cheeses. Locally, it is eaten alongside *kaymak*, rich unpasteurized double cream, with crumbly sheep feta, or by itself in specially designed cups that hold a single whole plum to be served alongside tiny cups of dark Turkish coffee.

**Production Area**
Bosnia-Herzegovina
Drina River Valley
Goradze

**Producers**
Five women

**Technical Partner**
Cooperativa Agropodrinje
(Bosnia-Herzegovina)

**Presidium Coordinators**
Paolo Bolzacchini
Tel. +39 02 38 10 20 60
paolo.bolzacchini@tiscali.it

Aida Zivojevic
Tel. +387 382 24198
cefa.g@bih.net.ba

**Presidium supported by**
Region of Tuscany

# Giant
# Istrian Ox

### The Great White 'Boscarin'

The Giant Istrian Ox, called 'Boscarin' in local dialect, is part of the extensive family of Podolican steers. The *Bos taurus macroceros*, which once populated the steppes of Easter Europe and Asia, is the grandfather of all the steppe cattle and the ancestor of the Istrian Ox. Podolican steer are named for Podolia, the granite-rich highlands of the Ukraine. The Istrian Ox is recognizable as an ancient breed simply by its massive size and great physical presence—the animal can easily weigh up to a metric ton. With their giant harp-shaped horns and white-gray mantles, these oxen are a majestic sight as they graze in the Croatian forests. The Istrian Ox is reared for milk, meat, and farm labor. This breed has been working the soil at least since Roman times and was one of the most important work animals of the Venetian Republic. During Venice's rule over the Adriatic, the city-state's government requisitioned some 20,000 oxen to tow oak logs from the high forests to port, where they were used to make thousands of war ships. The long train of oxen that pulled the logs from the forests down to Venice was called the *carrettada*, and the road on which they traveled linked the town of Montona with distant Portole in the San Marco woods.

At the time, the Venetian government mandated that the tops of the oak trees destined for shipbuilding be tied to the ground to make them grow in a bow shape. These enormous curved trunks were difficult to transport—their arched shape made them impossible to float them down the river—and sturdy animal traction was the only way to move them. The incredible strength of the area's white oxen was essential to Venetian shipbuilding and made the breed an asset to any small farm until the advent of the tractor.

Today, fewer and fewer Boscarin bulls are castrated—a necessary step to develop its full musculature—and the market for draft animals has all but disappeared. A market for ox meat has yet to emerge and breeders prefer to sell the young animals, earning some quick money instead of investing in the years needed to raise a mature animal.

## The Presidium

Of the 50,000 head counted before the Second World War, this breed has been reduced to near extinction: today only 200 exist in Istria. To save this genetic throwback, the use of the Boscarin Ox as a meat animal must be developed. The meat is flavorful, healthy, substantial and has market potential, but clearly the development of a market would entail a redevelopment of stock and a fair price. This is the objective of the project, which has been created thanks to the help of the Tuscan Cooperation Program. To this end, the Presidium will work on a project initiated by the Istrian Regional Authority to provide economic assistance to interested breeders and to increase the herds of Boscarin Oxen. In a second phase, when the oxen population is no longer 'at risk', the development of a gastronomic niche will become the priority.

**Production Area**
Croatia
Istria

**Producers**
15 breeders and an abattoir

**Presidium Coordinator**
Glauco Bevilacqua
Slow Food Convivium Leader
Tel. +385 98501357
comunitacittanova@hi.htnet.hr

**Presidium supported by**
Region of Tuscany

# Artisan
# Salted **Butter**

112

**Beyond Lurpak** Until the 1960s it was common for people in Denmark to buy their dairy produce in the local dairy, or *mejeri*. Butter used for everyday cooking was sold in small wooden casks or by weight. In all of Denmark there now are only 20 local dairies and the salted butter market is controlled by a single brand. Large-scale retailing is everywhere and even on the most remote islands, *Kro* (traditional Danish restaurants), are being replaced by pizzerias, Chinese or Italian restaurants. In this situation the production of high-quality dairy produce faces numerous obstacles, the supply of raw materials like top quality milk and unprocessed sea salt being the primary problem. The summer pastures which give the butter its rich, distinctive flavor, are becoming increasingly rare. The only saltworks left at this latitude hardly produce enough salt to supply a single dairy. In spite of this, some producers are still managing to keep traditional artisan methods alive. To make Artisan Salted Butter, whole milk is mechanically centrifuged to obtain cream, and an acidifying culture (each producer has his own recipe) is added. The mixture is allowed to acidify for a maximum of two days until the taste and smell of the mixture indicate that it is time to proceed to the churning stage. During this process the cream is churned, causing fat globules to break up and coalesce into butter, leaving residual buttermilk. The butter is manually removed from the churn and placed on a table, where a metal mold is used to divide it into 250-gram blocks with a characteristically irregular shape.

The shape of the blocks of Artisan Salt Butter and its variegated, hay-yellow color make it easy to distinguish it from industrial products. The scent alone is enough to distinguish one butter from another: Artisan Salted Butter is fragrant with a lingering scent of fresh cream and yogurt.

## Sweet and Sour

Butter can be made from sweet cream or sour cream, and while in America, England, and Italy we are accustomed to 'sweet cream butter', French and Scandinavians prefer butter made from slightly acidic cream, or 'cultured butter', the flavor of which is fuller and can have light overtones of sour milk or cheese.

Butter that is called 'salted' or that traditionally has a high percentage of salt, such as the Danish Jutland Peninsula butter or French Norman butter, is always cultured. The salt was added to stop runaway fermentation and ensure that the butter did not develop too much acidity. Historically, these butters were made from raw milk, which cultured naturally (in Europe only a few French AOC-designated producers continue to make raw-milk butter), but today they are made from pasteurized cream with the addition of freeze-dried cultures.

In addition to salting, to block against acidity, cultured butters are also washed after churning to rinse away excess lactic acid and make the butter more durable. Cultured butters have longer shelf life and resist higher temperatures than sweet cream butters, and they are better suited for savory foods than sweet cream butter.

## The Presidium

Lurpak Danish butter is one of the most highly visible high-quality butters on the international market. A global brand, it can be found in supermarkets from Southeast Asia to the Pacific Northwest. But Lurpak is not actually a producer of butter, but a brand under which almost all Danish butter is commercialized. This brand guarantees an acceptable quality standard, constant quality, and competitive prices, but imposes a standard style on producers. More significantly, all butter producers who choose not to adhere to the collective strategy and commercialize their own product suffer in this monopoly market. For this reason, the traditional *mejeri* are closing one by one.

Slow Food created this Presidium to address this problem, and to protect the centuries-old tradition of quality butter production. The ancient techniques used on the Jutland peninsula guarantee a pristine product of excellent quality. The concepts of local origin and gastronomic excellence are not widespread in Denmark, and for many consumers, the decision to purchase one butter instead of another is based on one single factor: its price. Therefore, the first objective of this project is to bring new attention to the quality of this product among local consumers.

| Production Area | Producers | Presidium Coordinator |
|---|---|---|
| Denmark Jutland Peninsula | One producer who sells through his *mejeri* | Kai Holm Jensen Tel. +45 26392898 kai&bente@fanonet.dk |

# Gascony Black Pig

## New Future for the *Noir*

The Gascony Black Pig is the most ancient breed of pig known in France. Similar to the Spanish Iberico, this breed is deep black in color and originated in the foothills of the French Pyrenees in the area around Nébouzanne, which stretches between the regions of Haute-Garonne, Haute-Pyrénées and Gers. This robust and vigorous breed can handle hot weather and fares best when raised free-range at pasture. The Gascony has small ears that stick out horizontally from the head and is an incredibly calm animal.

As with many rare breeds, the Gascony Black Pig grows much more slowly than most commercial breeds, increasing only 450 grams a day in weight, in contrast with the 800 grams a day of other modern breeds. This breed also has a much higher percentage of fat, with only 43% lean meat compared to an average of 56% among industrial breeds, and this abundant fat makes for exceptional flavor. The Gascony Black Pig is not adapted for intensive farming and therefore has been at risk of extinction, as farmers increasingly choose to maximize production over quality. In 1930, 28,000 head of Gascony Black Pigs grazed the pastures of the Pyrenees, while in 1970 only a few hundred remained. The breed was also losing genetic integrity due to frequent interbreeding. In 1981, 34 head of pure breed Gascony Black Pigs were documented, and at that point, a group of agricultural technicians and breeders decided to join together to save the breed.

The Gascony Black Pig continued to be highly at risk throughout the 1980s, above all because it was difficult to convince breeders to use an animal that grew so slowly and offered few economic incentives for its breeding. The challenge, therefore, was to find new commercial outlets that would encourage farmers to raise Gascony Black Pigs. In 1992, the cooperative of producers began producing salami and cured prosciutto, and because of this initiative, as well as the clear economic benefits for pig farmers, Gascony Black Pigs now number 600 head on 50 different farms.

The most important product made from the Gascony Black Pig is a cured whole ham, called Noir de Bigorre. These hams cure from 18 to 24 months and are served thinly hand-sliced at room temperature. The ham is fine-flavored with a warm, long-lasting scent and flavor.

Other specialties made from Gascony Black Pig include cured sausage and rolled bacon, both of which can be aged. The fresh meat of the Gascony Black Pig is also exceptional, and to best show its flavor, it should be cooked until just pale pink.

## The Presidium

There are 49 breeders and producers of cured meat in the Consortium du Noir de Bigorre. Noir de Bigorre has a product certification (CCP), which correlates with a production protocol that outlines rigid rules for production and animal husbandry. Although this same level of certification does not govern the production of cured sausage and bacon, these products are always made from the meat of animals raised free-range all year long at a population density of less than 25 head per hectare.

Today, the center that the producers founded to produce ham and other cured meats processes the pork of 4,000 pigs (not exclusively Gascony Black Pig), but must double that amount in order to become self-sufficient.

The objective of this Presidium is to continue to promote and conserve the Gascony Black Pig breed through products like the Noir de Bigorre *prosciutto*, cured sausages, and fresh meat.

| Production Area | Producers | Presidium Coordinators | Presidium supported by |
|---|---|---|---|
| France<br>Departments of Haute-Garonne and Haute-Pyrénées | 49 breeders and three producers of cured ham united in the *Consortium du Noir de Bigorre* | Didier Chabrol<br>Slow Food Convivium Leader<br>Tel. +33 467 45 10 72<br>didier@slowfood.fr<br><br>Armand Touzanne<br>Tel. +33 562348735<br>a.touzanne@hautes-piyrenees.chambagri.fr | Consortium du Noir de Bigorre |

# Pardailhan Black Turnip

## Reclaiming Roots

The plateau where Pardailhan is situated stands at an altitude of 800 meters above sea level, though it is just 40 kilometers from the Mediterranean. Although vineyards and olive groves are common to this region, the plain of Pardailhan is surrounded by pastures where cows and sheep graze and there are oak and beech forests thick with wild boar.

The quality of the Pardailhan Black Turnip has been celebrated for centuries, and at the end of the nineteenth century, it was sold at high prices at international fairs. After the Second World War, however, local agriculture slumped and the cultivation of these tubers declined. Only a few producers have conserved the tradition of growing Pardailhan Black Turnips and sell them exclusively in local markets in nearby towns like Béziers, Saint-Pons, and Narbonne.

Pardailhan Black Turnips are 'broadcast-seeded' at the beginning of August on well-worked land with one kilo of seed per hectare and left to wait for rain, which usually comes in the second half of the month. In autumn, the region's rain and heavy fog are very favorable for the turnip's growth: in Pardailhan it is said that the turnips 'drink from their leaves.' The farmers then handpick the turnips, starting in early November and ending in January.

Pardailhan Black Turnips are white inside, black outside and covered with numerous small roots. They can be recognized by the red clay residue that sticks to their skins. The Pardailhan Black Turnip is a variety called Caluire Long Black, named for its region of origin to the north of Pardailhan.

The Caluire Long Black has been acclimatized to Pardailhan for over a century (although seed stocks are regularly reinvigorated), and its flavor is considered unique thanks to the region's climate and soil. Pardailhain Black Turnips are beautifully tender with a subtle, sweet flavor, and must always be sliced lengthwise, following the root's natural fibers. They can be grated raw and tossed in a vinaigrette, fried in goose fat and a little sugar, or prepared in soups and gratins.

## Is French Cuisine too *Haute* for *Navet?*

Farmed for thousands of years in France, turnips—or *navets* in French—were once common throughout France. There were considered a staple: the residents of Limousin, for example, were called 'turnip eaters'. In France, turnip varieties abound and these humble tubers are strong representatives of their regions of origin. Today, the French eat less than a kilo of turnips a year, a quantity that diminishes with each passing year.

For the modern French, turnips seem somewhat unpalatable and unappealing. These irregularly-shaped tubers are often riddled with holes and other imperfections, offering fibrous flesh and sometimes a spicy flavor that the French are not accustomed to.

Traditionally, turnips are integral in *pot au feu*, a traditional dish that is increasingly rare. Escoffier wrote in his *Guide culinaire* (1903) that the turnip should be served as an accompaniment to duck, while twenty years later, Alain Ducasse, in his *Dictionnaire amoreux de la cuisine*, made no mention of the turnip at all.

Turnips have rarely been selected for production or taste by agricultural researchers. Their relatively aggressive flavor does not marry well with modern cuisine. Chefs today tend to substitute Japanese *daikon* radishes for turnips, a root that, although good when raw or pickled, lacks the lingering, bold earthiness of a well-cooked turnip.

## The Presidium

A long-term goal of the Presidium will be to encourage more producers to cultivate the Pardailhan Black Turnip (around 30–40 tons are grown annually), which will help rebuild the region's agriculture. The producers' association has created this Presidium to spread the word about their product. The 14 producers hope to redevelop some of the preserved turnip recipes for which Pardailhan was once famous, as today they are limited to selling for just three months of the year when the fresh product is available. They also intend to sell more in local markets. The town of Pardailhan, which numbers just 165 inhabitants, hosts an annual turnip festival that will expand to embrace Presidium promotional activities.

---

**Production Area**
France
Languedoc-Roussillon Department
Hérault Province
Pardailhan

**Producers**
14 farmers united in the
*Association des producteurs du Navet de Pardailhan*
(President, Elian Robert)

**Presidium Coordinators**
Didier Chabrol
Slow Food Convivium Leader
Tel. 33 467 45 10 72
didier@slowfood.fr

Elian Robert
Tel. +33 467 97 65 44
e.m.robert@cario.fr

**Presidium supported by**
Conseil général de l'Hérault

Parc Naturel Régional
du Haut-Languedoc

# Rennes Coucou Chicken

## Back from the Brink

Rennes Coucou Chicken is a local breed that was once widespread in Brittany, where it has been well known since the eighteenth century. In 1858, chicken specialist Charles Jaque described the breed in detail in his book, *Le Poulailler*, published by La Maison Rustique, and a certain Docteur Ramé, a local resident, dedicated his life to the selection and improvement that created the breed as we know it today. At the great Paris Agricultural Fair in 1903, the Rennes Coucou won best in show, and in 1914 the breed was registered and its characteristics defined. The Rennes Coucou's mostly gray feathers are streaked with blue and marked with regular bands of black and white.

The gradual decline of the Rennes Coucou began in 1950 and is linked to the industrialization of Brittany and to the development of more competitive meat-producing breeds. By the 1980s, the Rennes Coucou breed was considered nearly extinct. In 1988, the ecological museum of Rennes found a few surviving specimens and in 1989 brought together a group of farmers and enthusiasts to try to revive the breed. Thanks to this effort, it has slowly come back from the brink of extinction. The current breeders are dedicated to keeping the animal a rustic farmyard variety, raising it free-range with natural and foraged food. Today breeders include both amateurs and professionals and the Rennes Coucou is once again an important symbol of regional identity.

The characteristics of the Coucou Chicken that most pleased breeders were its hardiness, the quality of its meat, and its egg-laying ability. Today the Coucou is no longer used as a laying breed but is still prized for its hardiness and meat quality. This is a breed which grows slowly and produces firm yet tender meat with hints of hazelnuts. Its fine, supple, cream-colored skin adheres closely to the meat. The Rennes Coucou chicken is typically cooked in Brittany in apple cider and fresh cream.

## The Presidium

The association of Rennes Coucou Chicken Breeders has drafted and ratified a rigorous production protocol for all members. The birds are raised on open pasture (each has 10 square meters of terrain) for at least 130 days and no more than 500 are raised on one farm at one time. The feed is 100% vegetable-based, fortified with added minerals and vitamins, and all food sources are certified GMO-free. In the final 15 days before slaughter, the birds' feed is augmented with dairy products.

The eighteen producers of the association raise chickens year round, and a total of 25,000 Rennes Coucou are slaughtered per year. However, for all of the Coucou breeders these hens represent a side activity, not the primary one on their farms. Two-thirds of the Rennes Coucou hens reared are sold directly to restaurants by the producers' association. The other third is sold directly to consumers by individual breeders, either in markets or on farms.

The objective of the Presidium is to support the association of Coucou producers in their commercial relaunch of this rare breed, to help them maintain the high quality of their birds, and to spread the word about the excellent taste of their meat among interested consumers.

**Production Area**
France
Brittany and Pays-de-Loire Regions
Departments of Ille-et-Vilaine,
Morbihan and Loire-Atlantique

**Producers**
18 breeders united in the
*Association des producteurs de poulets Coucou de Rennes*
(President, Paul Renault)

**Presidium Coordinators**
Didier Chabrol
Slow Food Convivium Leader
Tel. +33 467 45 10 72
didier@slowfood.fr

Paul Renault
Tel. +33 2 99000590
www.coucouderennes.com

# Roussillon Dry Rancios Wine

## Oxidation Is a Must

Roussillon is a small French region that has been shaped as much by the culture of Spanish Catalonia as by that of France. Technically part of the eastern Pyrenees, it is France's southernmost province, and the famous mountain range is very much in evidence here, cresting above the region and plunging into the Mediterranean, right near the town of Banyuls. Grape vines grow along Collioure and Banyuls on the coast, as well as inland in Maury, Rivesaltes, and Côtes-du-Roussillon. Dry Rancios Wine is usually made with grenache or maccabeu grapes, the same used for making Banyuls, Maury, and Rivesaltes sweet wines.

This wine is a testimony of Roussillon's winemaking history: it was known as Banyuls before the laws changed regarding naturally sweet wines (those classed VDN in the French system). This change in laws allowed naturally sweet wines to be made with the addition of pure alcohol to stop the wine's natural fermentation, keeping some sugar in the wines, and making an irrevocable change in their traditional taste.

This wine is defined as dry because all of its sugars have been turned into alcohol. *Rancios* refers to the wine's aging in an environment that favors oxidation: in the open air and in open barrels. In order to cultivate pleasing flavors in these surroundings, it is essential that the wine have a high alcohol content.

Rancios wine is a far cry from many modern northern wines. It does not pair easily with food, and consumers—apart from Catalonians and the locals from Roussillon—are not used to its flavors. The few that appreciate its unique flavor drink it as an aperitif, to accompany tapas or salted anchovies. However, a Dry Rancios wine can easily substitute for Cognac or Armagnac at the close of a meal, and it heightens the enjoyment of a cigar. The flavor of the wine includes notes of toasted nuts, vanilla, licorice, and walnuts—all characteristics of the long aging in open barrels.

## The Presidium

The Roussillon Dry Rancios Wine producers' association was only formed recently and includes twelve winemakers. Production of this wine is minimal (10,000 liters annually), and it is almost impossibile to find in retail outlets. Actually, many wines of this type are excluded from commerce as laws prevent them from being labelled as wine because of their high alcohol content.

The Presidium was created to bring attention to this wine and to educate consumers interested in oxidized wines—especially in regions where this unusual flavor is appreciated as part of the gastronomic heritage. In the long term, the Presidium would like to work to overcome some of the legislative challenges blocking the commercialization of Roussillon Dry Rancios Wine.

**Production Area**
France
Languedoc-Roussillon Region
Pyrénées-Orientales Department

**Producers**
12 vinters united in the
*Association Les Rancios secs du Roussillon*

**Presidium Coordinators**
Didier Chabrol
Slow Food Convivium Leader
Tel. +33 467 45 10 72
didier@slowfood.fr

Brigitte Verdaguer
Tel. +33 468 29 03 47

**Presidium supported by**
Conseil général des
Pyrénées-Orientales

# Saint-Flour Planèze Golden **Lentil**

## A Legume from the Auvergne

The Saint-Flour Planèze basalt plateau varies in altitude between 800 and 1,200 meters and is hemmed in on its eastern and western sides by two mountain ranges, the Monts du Cantal on the west and Margeride on the east. These mountain ranges form a barrier that protect the Saint-Flour Planèze Golden Lentil fields from dominant winds and keep the plateau relatively temperate, given its altitude. The lowest areas of the plateau are used for cultivating cereals, peas and lentils. Documentation of the cultivation of the lentil in the area around Saint-Flour dates back to the late eighteenth century.

At the start of the twentieth century, 1,500 hectares of terrain cultivated with lentils produced 1,200 tons of the crop. The lentils were consumed locally and also sold and exported abroad. The production reached its apex in 1949, with 2,000 hectares of cultivated land.

But at the start of the 1970s, lentil production slowly lost ground to extensive livestock farming in the region due to the cultivation of forage necessary for feeding the animals, and almost became extinct. The area of the Auvergne where the lentil is grown is famous for Salers and

## The Presidium

The fifteen members of the Saint-Flour Planèze Golden Lentil producers' association farm 22 hectares of terrain, working to control quality, to stabilize minimum wholesale price, and to market the product.

The quality of the Golden Lentil depends on the soil in which it is grown. The preparation of the terrain, the harvest, and the threshing of the lentil plants are also extremely important phases of production and are thus very important to coordinate to ensure an excellent product.

The goal of the Presidium is to slowly increase the number of towns where the product is commercialized without compromising product quality. Given that the product is well known at a local level, the producers will work to expand beyond Saint-Flour into other areas of the Auvergne. In addition, the Presidium plans to produce a small booklet of traditional Golden Lentil recipes for chefs in the area.

Cantal cheeses and as their production increased, fields of lentils (the demand for which was decreasing in France) were sacrificed for milk production. The rediscovery and revival of the lentils began in 1997 through the work of producers who cultivated the fields around Saint-Flour. The scientific work of the selection of varieties for cultivation was accompanied by experimentation in the field by farmers trying out new agricultural techniques and by a group of tasters.

The memory of the golden Saint-Flour Lentil remains vivid for the elderly population of the town, and for this reason the newly revived product has found a local market. The lentil producers today are primarily animal breeders whose livelihoods are threatened by the extremely difficult milk market; the lentil offers a means of diversification, an additional resource, as well as a source of local pride.

Thanks to its fine, thin skin, this brown-streaked, yellow-green lentil cooks quickly and absorbs condiments and sauces well. It boasts a sweet flavor and a smooth texture that is never floury. Locally, the lentils are eaten as an accompaniment to pork or sausages or cold with a vinaigrette. There are also a few local recipes for puddings made with lentil flour.

**Production Area**
France
Auvergne Region
Cantal Department

**Producers**
15 farmers united in the *Association des producteurs de lentilles blondes et pois blonds du Pays de Saint-Flour* (President, Gérard Cibiel)

**Presidium Coordinators**
Didier Chabrol
Slow Food Convivium Leader
Tel. +33 467 451072
didier@slowfood.fr

Gérard Cibiel
Tel. +33 471 605009

**Presidium supported by**
Les communautés de communes du Pays de Saint-Flour et de la Planèze

# Mavrotragano

**A Tough Survivor**

When the *phylloxera* aphid devastated European vineyards in the late 1800s, it left few vines untouched. The vineyards of Santorini were among the rare exceptions; they were protected from infestation by the sandy, volcanic soil of the island. Unlike nearly every grape type in Europe, Santorini's Mavrotragano vines have never been grafted onto New World rootstock. Nevertheless, cultivation of Santorini's Mavrotragano production has shrunk considerably in the past fifty years, and the vine's low yield has led many to abandon viticulture for more lucrative options. The amount of acreage cultivated with Mavrotragano has been reduced by half since 1950.

Until recently, very few of the rare, red-grape Mavrotragano vines were cultivated, representing just 1% of the island's viticulture. Total production never exceeded 1,500 kilos, and Mavrotragano looked set for eventual disappearance.

Today, Mavrotragano's future looks brighter, thanks mostly to the work of two vintners who have revived the grape type and have developed techniques to increase the quantity of production. However, Mavrotragano cultivation will always be limited: the grapes are small, the bunches of average size, and yields are less than 40% than that of mandilarià, the only other red grape variety cultivated in Santorini's Cyclades region. Furthermore, the Mavrotragano matures in stages, requiring many mini-vintages throughout the year.

Mavrotragano grapes are grown particularly to produce red *passito* for consumption on special occasions. Wine enthusiasts know Santorini as a land of excellent white and sweet wines made from the better known assyrtiko grape, but the excellent quality of the red Mavrotragano has now attracted the attention of wine lovers in Greece and further afield.

Mavrotragano is harvested entirely by hand. The wine is fermented for nine days and subsequently stored in oak barrels for at least one year. Typical of southern wines, it is clear violet in color with an opulent and fruity aroma redolent of some of the wines of the southern Rhône valley. It has a spicy nose with notes of cinnamon and good tannins.

## Santorini

From above, the island of Santorini looks like a long strip of land curved like a seahorse in a placid, unbroken sea. When the sun sets here and the lamps blaze alight, the small white towns along the shore resemble tiny piles of salt against the steep black cliffs. At the center of the island, the volcano seems ready to reawaken from its sleep at any moment. The island's vineyards run low along the black soil as if to defend themselves from the strong and constant wind. The vineyards of Santorini are among the oldest on the globe, and have no equivalent elsewhere in the world—like many of the other foods produced on this island. These include sweet tomatoes, once primary materials for a booming conserves industry; white eggplants; and Santorini fava beans, which, unlike their name suggests, are tiny small beans that are hulled by hand with mule-driven hullers and buried underground to age for a year.

### The Presidium

This Presidium will support the activity of the two extant producers, Paris Sigalas and Haridimos Hadjidakis, who have saved Mavrotragano and have convinced many small Santorini producers to plant the variety.

The Presidium is building on the fundamental work begun by Sigalas and Hadjidakis, and its objective is to involve other producers, to increase output, and to set out guidelines for production, which will guarantee the quality of the product. Insieme (a group of Piedmontese red wine producers) recently visited the area of production and have begun to provide technical assistance and collaboration.

Saffron gatherer and fisherman depicted in frescoes from 3000 BCE found at Akotiri, the ancient capital of Santorini

| Production Area | Producers | Presidium Coordinators |
|---|---|---|
| Greece<br>Eastern Santorini Island | Two winemakers | Evelyn and George Hatziyiannakis<br>Slow Food Convivium Leader<br>Tel. +30 2286022249<br>selenegr@otenet.gr |

# Which Wines Become Presidia?

There are thousands of varieties of *Vitis vinifera*, but only fifty make up 95% of the world's production. In Italy, for example, there are nearly 350 vine varieties registered at the provincial level, but of these only three hundred are 'cultivated', and many at such low levels as to be unviable commercially. There are many wine grape varieties in Italy and around the world that are at risk of extinction—are these all possible candidates for Presidia? Obviously, not all, as many forgotten varieties are not commercially viable and some are of mediocre quality, even though in many cases they are linked to rural identity and ancient winemaking traditions. Therefore, the Presidia project has always approached the world of wine with great care: there are just too many interests at stake and too much local pride. For now we have selected only five wines and one wine-based product: Mavrotragano of Santorini, a red variety that is described by its Greek name as 'bitter and crunchy'; Roussillon Dry Rancios Wine, an oxidated wine not protected by the French *appellation controleè* (unlike the more well-known and profitable sweet Rancios), the Schiacchetrà of Cinque Terre, Trentino Vino Santo and Bagnarlo Moscato Passito. Another Presidia 'wine' is Saracena Moscato, which does not legally qualify as a wine because it requires production techniques that are relics of Italy's Arab invasion, in which generic varieties of cooked must is added to the juice of moscatello grapes that have been

left to wither.

This group is not casually chosen: there is a common thread that connects these varied products. Aside from having exceptional and unusual taste qualities, their production techniques are sustainable. From the Ligurian terraced vineyards to the historic valleys of Piedmont, from the Homeric cultivation of a Greek island suffocating under tourism to the meticulous techniques of a unique production in the deepest south of Italy—all these Presidia portray more strongly than anything else how territory, history, and ancient flavors can continue to thrive.

# Niotiko

## Unseen Ios

Ios is part of the Cyclades Islands, just an hour by ferry from Santorini. In the past few years, it has become a cult destination for thousands of twentysomethings who fill the island's discos and bars all summer long. But if you leave the beach resorts and head inland, it is like stepping back into an earlier, more rustic past. The island's interior is filled with uninhabited mountains covered in low brush, crosscut by ancient stone walls and steep curving cart tracks.

Some four thousand goats roam this tranquil interior region, the silence here broken only by the movement of goatherds and their flocks. Just twenty of the goatherds on Ios continue to produce the island's rustic local cheese, which, in Greek, means 'from Ios.' In Greece, where every island produces its own cheese, all the local varieties are inevitably distinguished simply by their provenance.

Niotiko is a simple rustic cheese. Raw goat milk is mixed with a splash of cow or sheep milk (if any is on hand) and curdled with goat rennet, often handmade from the goatherd's kids. The preparation technique is as simple as cheesemaking can get: the curd is broken with a forked wooden stick and left to settle to the bottom of the vat. Then it is collected with a slotted scoop and piled into hand-made molds. After salting, the cheese is left to age in a stone cellar. The leftover whey is mixed with fresh milk and boiled to make *mizitra*, a fresh, soft, ricotta.

Niotiko's flavors recall the aromatic herbs of the Mediterranean scrub: wild sage, thyme, and pine. It also offers slightly mineral notes, underscored by hints of the salty sea air of the Cyclades. This round cheese has a deep yellow crust and a white curd. Niotiko tastes pleasingly rich with a creamy consistency. After two or three months in the cellar, it develops a fuller taste. Niotiko is an essential and simple cheese, both in production and in flavor. With its sunny, wild, marine flavors, it perfectly expresses the characteristics of the island of Ios, and can be aged for an exceptionally long time at warm temperatures. In fact, Jason's Argonauts may well have eaten a cheese like this on their long voyage.

### The Presidium

The Presidium will endeavor to join the shepherds into a cooperative to establish the best aging procedures, so ensuring a market for this ancient product. In this way pastoral farming can survive and Ios's rural culture may have a future. Niotiko is already produced in full accordance with some of the rules governing Presidium cheeses. It uses only raw milk, has no added bacteria to accelerate flavor development, the animals are kept on pasture, and only natural products are used as additional feed. The Presidium aims to help the cheesemakers introduce their own brand name and label, which will identify the name of the producer, the type of raw milk used and, if possible, the breed of goat providing the milk.

## Challenging Cheese

Is there such thing as an ideal Presidium? One where, upon arrival in the project's location, one discovers the producers get along wonderfully, sell in plenty of markets, and all their products are uniformly excellent? This does not, in fact, exist—and if it did, there would be no need for the Presidia projects at all.

Niotiko, for example, is a goat cheese produced by twenty cheesemakers in the rocky midlands of Ios, one of the most beautiful islands of the Aegean. The idea for a Presidium for Niotiko, which was suggested by the tireless Convivium leaders of Santorini, presents an intriguing image of this lush green island, with its 5,000 goats grazing unbeknownst to the thousands of young people vacationing on the beaches, in stark contrast with the families that make their living from farming and cheesemaking.

At times, Niotiko tastes rustic, elemental and good. Other times, the cheese is salty, acidic and defective—a perfect example of the inconsistencies in many rural shepherds' products. Ios is an isolated island; it is one hour's ferry ride from Santorini, itself an hour by plane from Athens. The shepherds here speak only Greek and they prefer traditional wisdom about cheesemaking to European Union sanitation regulations.

The dynamic, enthusiastic mayor of Ios believes in his land and that its yield will prove satisfactory. 'We need to construct a single modern dairy,' he proposed to Slow Food, 'to collect the milk, and then we will have a steady supply.' This would mean eradicating an extraordinary part of the biodiversity of the local culture. The motive for the mayor's extreme stance was that Niotiko cheese currently does not satisfy hygiene laws and cannot be legally sold. As an alternative, the Presidium contacted a dairy technician, a Cypriot, the only one available to travel into the mountains of the island. Photis Papademas first went to a meeting of twenty shepherds who regarded him with suspicion. He then visited five breeders over the course of the week, preparing an analysis of production and identifying crucial aspects of production, including salting, aging, the ratio of goat to sheep milk (when writing the production protocol, the cheesemakers excluded the use of cow's milk, which had previously been incorporated).

Luca Nicolandi, a veterinarian, traveled to Ios two months later to ascertain what progress had been made. The next steps will be slow, but Niotiko may soon be able to be exported to mainland Greece and around Europe while retaining its traditionality.

| Production Area | Producers | Presidium Coordinators | Presidium supported by |
|---|---|---|---|
| Greece | Five cheesemakers and | Evelyn and George Hatziyiannakis | Consorzio Tutela |
| Ios Island | shepherds | Slow Food Convivium Leader | Vino Lessini Durello |
| | | Tel. +30 2286022249 | |
| | **Technical Partner** | selenegr@otenet.gr | |
| | AVEC - Veterinary Association for | | |
| | Cooperation in Developing | Costas Rodopoulos | |
| | Countries | Municipality of Ios | |
| | | Tel.+30 22860 91935 | |
| | | tadepi@mail.otenet.gr | |

# Mangalica Sausage

## Sweet Cured Sausage Rich with Paprika

The Mangalica pig breed (also called Mangaliza or Mangalitsa) was once found across Hungary and in bordering countries, particularly Romania. The corpulent Mangalica grows very slowly and cannot be kept in closed quarters. It is therefore poorly suited to modern industrial pig farms, and it has been gradually replaced by modern breeds. The pig is distinguished by its rich and curly coat, which is usually blond, sometimes black, and occasionally red. On the Hungarian plains, farmers raise Mangalica pigs free-range and feed them a mix of wild pasture, supplemented with potatoes and pumpkins produced on the farm.

This flavorful pork can be braised slowly in the oven or cooked in stock. Sauerkraut, potatoes, and stuffed peppers are the usual accompaniments. Mangalica breeders also cure their own smoked hams and sausages according to traditional techniques. The sausage, the primary product made from this pig, is produced in various forms and sizes, but the most traditional type is packed in the pig's duodenum and has a diameter of about three centimeters and a length that can reach 70 centimeters. To make the sausage, the meat is minced finely with the animal's lard using an electric grinder and seasoned with salt, pepper, sweet paprika, and other spices, depending on the producer's particular recipe. The sausages are stuffed into casings by hand and cold-smoked over an acacia- or oak-wood fire and are then left to age—ideally for at least two or three months. Traditionally, this cured sausage is eaten in slices accompanied by pickled vegetables such as cucumbers or peppers stuffed with cabbage. The sweet paprika used to season the sausage gives the final product a natural sweetness and a vibrant red color.

**The Presidium**   This Presidium was created to bring attention to an ancient breed of pig, ideal for sausage making because of its excellent and fatty meat. The producers who still make Mangalica Sausage are a small, dedicated and well-organized group. The eleven pig farmers have formed a cooperative and are certified organic. All the producers are found in the Kinkusag region just south of Budapest at the center of one of the most important national parks in the country. These farmers raise the pigs, produce sausages and hams in-house, and even produce their own paprika to season their sausages.

The Presidium is working to help this group promote their product by gradually increasing the number of animals raised and intends to bring together other groups of Hungarians who are trying to save this breed.

| Production Area | Producers | Presidium Coordinators | Presidium supported by |
|---|---|---|---|
| Hungary Kinkusag Region | Eleven breeders and sausage makers united in an association, all certified organic | Gabor Lövei Tel. +45 58113436 Gabor.Lovei@agrsci.dk<br><br>Olga Rendek Tel. +36 76710962 | Scandicci Slow Food Convivium |

# Paprika, Cayenne, and Everything in Between

Paprika is as ubiquitous in Hungarian cuisine as the tomato in the Mediterranean, seasoning everything from meat to soup, to vegetables. It is used to make most traditional cured sausages, imbuing them all a vivid red color.

Brought to Hungary by the Turks after the battle of Mohàcs in 1526, when they conquered the Hungarian Empire, the peppers farmed across the country were of the *Capsicum annuum* species, the favorite of the Hungarians as well as the Middle Easterners, as it was the most fragrant pepper on the market.

Paprika first appeared on the Hungarian market in the mid-1500s, and since that time, the mix of pepper powder of varying intensity has been one of the strongest symbols of the cultural identity of the country. The most famous paprika is produced around the city of Segez, but many farming families across Hungary make it as well. Peppers came to Europe aboard Christopher Columbus' ships returning from the New World. 'There are *axi* in abundance,' wrote Columbus, 'and their pepper is much better than that of pepper itself'. *Axi* was the indigenous name for peppers, but as soon as *axi* landed in Europe they were baptized 'Indian peppers', a misnomer that exists—in part—to this day.

Domesticated in Mexico around 3500 BCE, peppers were cultivated and used by the Aztecs as food and medicine. In contrast to other American plants like the tomato and potato, which endured years of general neglect before they were included in the European larder, Continentals eagerly embraced peppers.

Peppers were considered a useful substitute for peppercorns and other spices that were impossible to find or simply too expensive.

Their immediate success killed the hopes of the Spanish monarchy (and of Columbus himself) to start a lucrative commercial monopoly. Unfortunately for them, peppers adapted well to the European climate and spread quickly.

From Europe, the pepper traveled to Africa and then to the Far East, where it became an indispensable ingredient. Today, there is no country in the world where the pepper is not cultivated, varying only in name depending on provenance, of which paprika, red pepper, cayenne pepper, Guinea pepper, and chili pepper are just a few.

All together, 26 species are documented, but *Cap. annuum* (e.g. Jalapeno, Cayenne), *Cap. frutescens* (e.g. Tabasco), *Cap. chinensis* (e.g. Habañero), *Cap. baccatum* (e.g. Cappello del Vescovo or Bishop Crown) and *Cap. pubescens* (e.g. Rocoto) are the most commonly cultivated. In Mexico, which has the greatest diversity of edible peppers, cooks pride themselves on their secret combinations of pepper varieties that are used to make traditional dishes. In the Western Hemisphere, this level of secrecy is still uncommon, and varieties are cultivated based only on level of spiciness.

Spiciness is measured by a system established by American chemist Wilbur Scoville in 1912. This scale, measured in Scoville Units, assigns a value to a level of spiciness based on the amount of water needed to dilute capsaicin, the 'spicy' element of pepper, to neutrality. The Scoville rating varies from 0-150 cc. of water for a generic sweet pepper to 350 liters of water for a hot pepper like the Habañero Red Savina.

# Irish Raw Cow Milk Cheese

## Protecting New Traditions

Four centuries ago, Ireland had over four hundred types of traditional cheese. Today, all that remains are their Celtic names: Tanach, Grus, Faiscre, Grotha, Gruth, Tàth, Millsén, Maotha and Mulchàn. Today no one knows what Tanach or Millsén looked like, how Faiscre or Grus was made, or how much a form of Grotha or Gruth or Maotha weighed. There is only the legacy of their nomenclature, which has been copied down from inventory lists and a few literary references.

Beginning in the sixteenth century, increasingly restrictive laws enforced by Ireland's English rulers reduced the Irish to the supply end of a mercantilist economy, producing pork, oats, and butter for England and her colonies. With laws strictly stipulating that exports and taxes be paid to English landlords in foodstuffs, Irish food producers no longer had enough milk to produce their own cheese. Cheese had been a staple of the Celtic diet, but the grip of English colonial law slowly reduced the Irish diet to potatoes and little else. In the twentieth century, Irish governments have tried to establish various types of cheese industries; to this end, federally supported factories producing Camembert, Gruyère, and Cheddar were established.

In the 1970s, a loose association of artisans began to reintroduce cheesemaking on a small scale in rural Ireland, and this soon swelled to 30 small dairies. Of these, only a dozen have survived the past decade as Ireland has some of the most rigid laws regulating raw milk cheesemaking. Many producers have abandoned cheesemaking as they are unwilling to endure constant and costly hygiene checks or requests to carry out extreme measures (weekly cleaning of the aging cave with bleach, for example).

The approach of the Irish health authorities is provoked by the wave of food scandals in the UK in recent years. Even more so, they are bolstered by the absence of traditional foods, which in turn results in a lack of respect for traditional production methods. Ireland has been more hesitant than other European countries in designating appellations (PDO, PGI) to protect artisan food like those common in Britain, France, and Italy.

## The Presidium

True symbols of national identity, Irish cheeses are once again at risk of extinction—this time, due to restrictive legislation governing raw milk production. The Presidium is made up of fifteen artisan producers who work with artisan techniques that vary from one to the next. Jeffa Gill's Durrus cheese has a lightly washed crust and an intense scent of green leaves and forest undergrowth, while Bill Hogan's Desmond cheese is a large hard cheese made in the Swiss style with a crumbly texture and, scents of the forest, notes of walnuts, and a spicy concluding note.

The Presidium's dual objectives are to defend the right of small producers to make raw milk cheese in Ireland, and to promote the consumption and understanding of these innovative artisan cheeses.

## West Cork's Flower Children

In the 1970s, a group of ex-city dwellers and a few expatriates moved to the bluffs and headlands of West Cork in southwest Ireland to try their hands at farming. They were looking to live close to the land, to get away from it all in a last upswing of '60s counterculture energy, and cheesemaking offered them the possibility to farm while producing something creative. West Cork's neo-cheesemakers (eight in all) began producing a range of cow's milk cheeses, primarily washed rind. They learned to make cheese by studying a few weeks in France or England, or at times simply by reading specialized books and filling in the gaps by trial and error. Many of the Presidia producers are in this group of 'revolutionaries', although some of the original group of eight have had to stop producing raw milk cheese under pressure from the government's raw milk legislation. Jeffa Gill was one of the first of the group to move to the countryside. She came to West Cork after fashion school in Dublin and developed her washed-rind Durrus cheese through a decade of trial and error. Like many of her generation, making cheese initially seemed like just one part of a lifestyle choice, not a profession. As Jeffa says, "It took me several years before I realized I was actually going to *be* a cheesemaker."

| Production Area | Producers | Presidium Coordinator |
|---|---|---|
| Ireland<br>County Cork and the Midlands | 15 cheesemakers | Kevin Sheridan<br>Tel. +353 469430373<br>kevin@sheridanscheesemongers.com |

# Irish Wild
# Smoked Salmon

## Just Salt, Smoke and Salmon

Generations have described Irish coastal waters as being 'alive with salmon', and some even claimed that their numbers were once so many that you could almost walk the water on their shimmering, silvery skins. Today, the salmon are not as thick in the water, and without a concerted effort to promote sustainable fishing, Irish waters risk losing their legendary wealth.

Today, small in-shore commercial fishermen fish wild salmon in a 36-day period between June 1 and July 31. The Presidium salmon produced by the four Irish smokers is based only on wild salmon fished from local inshore and in-harbor waters. Their wild catch is precious. Rare and flavorful, fresh wild salmon appears to be a solid pink muscle enveloped in silver skin.

Ireland's coastal inhabitants have been transforming fresh salmon into a smoked and long-lasting food for as long as the island has been inhabited. The treatment and processing of wild salmon is an essential process that respects the integrity of its natural flavor, and the process has changed little with the passage of centuries. The artisan smoked salmon producer relies on the balance and interplay of fish, sea salt, and oak or beech smoke, and the understanding of the craftsman is essential in determining the equilibrium of the final product through the cleaning, salting, and smoking of the fish. The producers of the Irish Wild Smoked Salmon Presidium are united by their high-quality product but retain essential differences: Anthony Creswell adds a dash of sweet raw sugar to his brine; Frank Hederman smokes over chipped beech, sometimes from aged whiskey barrels; while Peter Dunn and Sally Barnes use a dry salt cure to create more intense flavors.

## The Presidium

In recent years, the upsurge in salmon farming stands as a haunting portent of the large-scale domestication of a wild species, potentially mirroring the intensification of livestock farming. The Presidium producers support the promotion of sustainable fishing, and actively support ecological programs to help maintain the salmon ecosystem of Ireland's rivers. Above all, Anthony, Frank, Peter, and Sally are working to develop understanding of Ireland's precious resource, from both an ecological and a gastronomic point of view.

For more information on the ecological role of Irish salmon populations and on the Presidium's environmental work, contact the project's scientific advisor, Mark Boyden, streamscapes@eircom.net.

| Production Area | Producers | Presidium Coordinator | Presidium supported by |
|---|---|---|---|
| Ireland | Four salmon smokers | Anthony Creswell | Febvre & Co |
| | | Tel. +353 23 46644 | |
| | | info@ummera.com | |

# Aged Artisan Gouda

## Too Good to be 'Gouda'

The town of Gouda became a central cheese market in the seventeenth century, and the first weighing rights were granted in 1668. Farmers and traders were obliged to weigh their cheeses here and taxes were imposed. Records from that time show that at least a million kilos of farmstead cheese were traded that year. In the northern parts of the Netherlands, dairy cooperatives took over cheese production from individual farmers in the late 1800s. Fortunately, the Gouda cheesemakers resisted this trend, and traditional farmstead cheesemaking has persisted till today.

Some 300 farmers in The Netherlands, most of them in the Gouda region, still produce raw milk farmstead cheese (called *boerenkaas*). Their numbers are shrinking due to the expansion of urban areas, increased production costs, hygiene restrictions and the abundance of cheap pasteurized imitations.

Boeren-Goudse Oplegkaas, as Aged Artisan Gouda is called in Dutch, is made from raw milk only during the summer season, when cows are grazed on the open pastures of the peat meadows or *polders* of the Green Hart region, between the cities of Amsterdam, Rotterdam and Utrecht. Boeren-Goudse Oplegkaas cheeses must age for at least one year but can age up to four years (*opleg* means 'aged' in Dutch).

Like all Gouda, Boeren-Goudse Oplegkaas is a washed-curd cheese. Washing the curd removes part of the lactose, which reduces the possibility that acidity and bitterness build up in the aged forms. The cheesemaking starts with the warm milk of the morning's milking, which is mixed with a starter culture made on the farm.

Authentic Boeren-Goudse Oplegkaas is peerless in taste, with a sweet mild flavor that blooms in the mouth, a well-structured aftertaste with a light acidity and the warm caramel taste that characterizes most Gouda. Its dense curd remains creamy and full even after it has been stored three or four years on wooden shelves.

### The Presidium

Gouda is too often a banal cheese, its familiar thickly wax-coated forms available on supermarket shelves around the world. This is the impetus behind this Presidium's work to save the finest quality version of the cheese: Boeren-Goudse Oplegkaas, which is made by three farmers who graze their Fresian cattle (although most Fresian raised in the Netherlands are slightly smaller than their cousins we see elsewhere in Europe) on the low polder fields surrounding the city of Gouda. The cheesemakers (traditionally farmers' wives) make the cheeses, each weighing over 20 kilograms, in traditional wooden molds lined with natural linen. The crust of this yellow cheese forms naturally with a minimal use of plastic. The producers are currently seeking to phase out the use of substances on the rind that control molds.

In the Netherlands, farmstead cheesemakers have depended for centuries on wholesalers who age the cheeses and resell them without citing the name of the producer. Slow Food is working to offer an alternative by organizing a fairer way of commercialization. Producers and Slow Food promote the aged *Boeren-Goudse Oplegkaas* directly to consumers.

| Production Area | Producers | Presidium Coordinator |
|---|---|---|
| The Netherlands | Three cheesemakers | Marjolein Kooistra |
| Green Hart Region | | Tel. +31 10 4678762 |
| | | goudseboerenkaas@hotmail.com |

# Eastern Scheldt Lobster

## Zeeland's Rare *Homarus*

A deep bay on the Zeeland coast of Holland on the North Sea, the Eastern Scheldt (known as the Oosterschelde in Dutch) was once an estuary. Dams constructed over the course of the past two centuries blocked the influx of fresh water from the river. The estuary became a bay, and new populations of oysters and lobsters (*Homarus gammarus,* their common name is European Lobster) moved in to join the local mussel populations.

The lobsters first flourished in the bay's ideal habitat, but by the turn of the century over-fishing had driven them nearly to extinction. In the 1960s, a severely cold winter killed all but the hardiest specimens. Today the Eastern Scheldt Bay is a closed habitat due to the dams and dikes built around its perimeter, and the lobsters enclosed within have evolved into a unique and thriving sub-species. The Eastern Scheldt Lobster differs from Canadian and American lobsters in its deep blue color and the red-orange spots that mark its claws. Like North American lobsters, it turns deep red when cooked, but the flavor and texture of the flesh differs slightly between continents. The meat of the Eastern Scheldt European Lobster is whiter and slightly softer than that of North American crustaceans. *Homarus gammarus* lives hidden between the rocks and stones of the numerous dams and dikes along the Eastern Scheldt, from the low water line down to depths of fifty meters below sea level. Lobsters need six years or more to reach maturity, and while many slow growing fish species have become rare due to over-fishing, local fishermen are working to make sure this does not happen to the lobsters of the Eastern Scheldt. The fishing season is short, lasting from April 1 to July 15, and fishing is small-scale and strictly regulated.

## Spidery and Delicious, but are they Sustainable Seafood?

Crustaceans are an intersection of spider and fish, their segmented bodies recall other arthropods', but their tender, delicious flesh tastes of their marine habitat. Lobsters, crayfish, shrimp, and crab have been appreciated for centuries and all are in recipe books dating from the sixteenth century. At that time, they were considered rare delicacies or even aphrodisiacs. The Presidia have identified a number of excellent crustaceans around the world, as well as the small groups of artisan fishermen who fish them sustainably, using traditiional methods. The ancient techniques used by the Presidia producers are selective and do not sweep up by-catch, but are designed to capture one specific variety. These include the cone-shaped straw nets, called *nasse*, that are used by Italian fishermen in Campania, as well as the Dutch *fulken*, which have a similar design. The Venetian *vieri* capture only soft-shell crabs, and the wooden cages used in Chile to catch lobster and golden crab are other examples of selective fishing—where just the right crustaceans are captured.

## The Presidium

The Eastern Scheldt Lobster Presidium recognizes a sustainable low-impact fishing system and a uniquely well-organized and responsible group of small artisan producers. They fish using baited conical nets and carefully return small lobsters and females with eggs to the bay to form the basis for lobster fishing for years to come. Male lobsters longer than 24 centimeters are taken on board in seawater tanks and are sold fresh. The Eastern Scheldt Lobster Foundation has worked together with fishermen and volunteers over the past few years to promote this sustainable and low-impact system within their local community. Every year, they celebrate the opening of the lobster season in the town of Zierikzee with a festival and have also involved a number of restaurants in the area that support the consumption of local lobsters instead of imported fish.

| Production Area | Producers | Presidium Coordinator |
|---|---|---|
| The Netherlands | Five fishermen that collaborate | Balth Roessingh |
| Zeeland | with the Foundation for the | Tel. +31 111 644030-653 353843 |
| Eastern Scheldt | Eastern Scheldt Lobster | info@jcom.nl - schute@haansbeijsens.nl |
| | | www.oosterscheldekreeft.nl |

# Texel Sheep Cheese

## A Landscape Formed by the Elements

The flat green island of Texel is surrounded by the endless vista of the steel grey North Sea. The wind that sweeps over the island is so strong and constant that the roofs of the island's barns are sloped on one side to reduce resistance—they look as if they are kneeling into the gale. The island of Texel has given its name to a famous sheep breed, which, with its broad shoulders, thick neck and short legs, is also built in a way that suggests sturdy resistance to the elements.

Texel sheep are among the most common in the world, and breeders are spread across the United Kingdom, Denmark, the United States, Brazil, Ireland, and even Italy. Before 1850, however, there was a different type of Texel sheep, raised not for meat, but for milk. This breed was slowly selected for meat production as the island began to produce lamb and mutton for export to the United Kingdom. As a result, the island's traditional production of Texel cheese, known as Texelse Schapenkaas, slowed to a halt. Texel's cheese had been known throughout Europe, and in 1567 the Italian traveler Ludovico Guicciardini wrote that

Until recently, the Bakkers were the only farmers who produced Texel Sheep Cheese with the traditional recipe. After contact with Slow Food, a second producer, Anton Witte, decided to return to raw milk cheese production and joined the new Presidium. The two producers make cheese with natural rennet and raw milk, preferably from Texelaar-Friesian sheep. The goal of the Presidium is to help Texelse Schapenkaas regain its reputation for quality and to encourage additional farmers to adopt the quality standards of the Presidium. With sheep milk cheese complementing the poor incomes from lamb production, many endangered farms can be saved and can then reinforce the island's rural economy. Sheep are part of the typical Texel landscape's hedged pastures and play an important role in preserving the island's ecosystem by grazing the salt-resistant vegetation of Texel's loamy peat meadows.

the islanders of Texel 'make cheeses... of a particularly delicate taste, which no other cheese, not even the Parmesan, can be compared with.'

After the Second World War, the production of Texel was drastically reduced and with it the artisan cheese with at least five centuries of history disappeared. In the early eighties, one farming family revitalized the island's tradition. Piet and Hanna Bakker relaunched production with the help of an aunt's recollections of how the cheese was once made. One problem the Bakkers faced was the local sheep breed: Texel sheep had been selected for meat production for a century and a half, and no longer yielded much milk. The Bakkers crossed their sheep with Fresian milk sheep again and made a selection of good milking ewes: after a decade they came up with a Texel-Fresian (called Texelaar-Friesian) cross that was a good milk producer.

The fresh cheeses weigh between four and five kilos and are aged a minimum of six months. The cheese is rustic and has a lingering elemental flavor that tastes of animal musk and the sea. The cheese's deep yellow color is evidence of Texel's rich and abundant pasture. Texel is produced by partially cooking and never washing the curd, a technique that is unusual for the Netherlands,

| Production Area | Producers | Presidium Coordinator |
|---|---|---|
| The Netherlands Texel Island | Two cheesemakers | Hielke van der Meulen Tel. +31 317 427500 hielke.vandermeulen@hetnet.nl |

# Oscypek

### Smoked Sheep Spindles from the Tatra Mountains

Oscypek has been produced in the Tatra mountains since the fourteenth century, when farmers from the southern Romanian province of Walachia imported dairy farming to the Polish region of Carpazi. Oscypek is a sheep's milk cheese made from the milk of Zackel sheep, a Hungarian breed that has acclimated perfectly over the past three or four centuries.

Until recently, the production area for this cheese was limited to the Tatra mountains, but with the inception of the region's National Park—when the regions of Pieniny, Gorce, Beskidy and Bieszcady were conserved and made available for grazing—the area of production has grown to include the park. The Tatra mountains vary in altitude between 800 and 1,500 meters. Despite abundant rainfall, the pastures are not rich in forage because the temperature remains low throughout the year. The sheep are kept outside from May to September and are milked twice a day. The cheese is produced by the shepherds themselves in rudimentary—but rigorously clean—huts. In the huts, a fire is always lit; it is used for the cheesemaking and for smoking the finished cheeses that are hung from the rafters.

The most notable aspect of these smoked, hard cheeses is their shape, spindle-like with a decorative band impressed into the circumference. The first step in producing Oscypek is the heating of the raw sheep milk from the morning and evening milkings. Next, the milk is mixed with calf rennet. After a first cutting of the curds, hot water is added, and the curds are broken a second time. The mass is then worked by hand into the typical spindle shape. To give the cheese this unusual form, the cheesemaker works the curd slowly between his skilled hands, adding warm water occasionally to keep the curd soft. Each form of Oscypek requires at least an hour of manual manipulation, as the cheesemaker gently kneads the cheese and presses out the excess whey. With a wooden ring, the cheeses are embossed with the characteristic mark of every producer and salted for 24 hours. Then they are hung from the beams to be smoked.

When mature, Oscypek weighs between 600 and 800 grams, and is eight or nine centimeters in diameter. The cheese is compact with a pale straw-yellow color, offering a clean, lightly toasted aroma with pleasant mineral notes and a chestnut flavor. Oscypek is usually served in thin slices accompanied by wine, vodka or beer. It is also excellent grilled.

## The Presidium

This Presidium is working to spread knowledge and appreciation of this unique Eastern European cheese. Eventually, the Presidium may extend to include an important secondary product: the exceptionally tender, flavorful meat of the lambs of the local sheep breed. The project's primary objective is to promote this product within the region, particularly to the best restaurants of Krakow and Warsaw. Also, given Poland's recent entry into the European Union, Oscypek could also become an important agricultural export.

**Production Area**
Poland
Tatra Mountains

**Producers**
Five cheesemaker-shepherds

**Presidium Coordinator**
Jacek Szklarek
Slow Food Convivium Leader
Tel. +48 509 093034
jacek.szklarek@tosca.com.pl

**Presidium supported by**
Twenty-three Roero Wine Producers

# Polish Mead

## Drinkable Honey

Mead, along with vodka, was once prepared in all Polish homes. Today, few producers remain, and only one mead maker in all Poland still uses the traditional recipe. This producer, Maciej Jaros, is a giant of a man with huge hands, blue eyes, and a droopy handlebar mustache. Jaros lives a few kilometers from Warsaw and has made mead commercially in his family business ever since the Polish government removed the ban on small private enterprise in 1991.

In his small workshop, Jaros keeps an apiary of thirty hives that produce a dark yellow and aromatic honey, and he believes that the best honeys for mead are heather or fir. "If you don't know how to make honey, you cannot make mead," explains Jaros. "You have to know your materials to make the finest mead." Many types of mead exist, varying in quality according to the proportion of honey to water—from one part honey to three parts water, to two parts honey to one part water. The latter version, called *pultorak*, is the most precious. The more honey used to make the mead, the longer it can be aged. The minimum aging time is four to five years, but bottles aged 15 and even 20 years still exist.

The preparation of Polish Mead begins by boiling honey and water mixed with local herbs. The mixture is then fermented and aged in large stainless steel barrels. Some varieties of Polish Mead are traditionally flavored with raspberry, apple, or grape juice.

The authentic recipe for Polish Mead has been saved by generations of artisans and was given to Jaros by his mother, one of the few people still alive who knew how to achieve the exact balance between flavor and aroma. Traditionally, women always produced the mead, while men were responsible for the apiaries.

The hand-made ceramic bottles in which Polish Mead is sold are also characteristic of the product. Glass was often too expensive for poor families, and they baked their own jug-like bottles in small kilns.

## The Presidium

Jaros, like all traditional mead producers, makes the honey from which his mead is made, the mead itself and even the clay vessels in which the mead is bottled. Jaros's mead is completely different from the industrial mead that can be found everywhere on the Polish market. Young mead's relative tastelessness is compensated for with the addition of artificial aromas. To make quality mead, it is critical to begin with good ingredients and ample time, as the product needs to age six or seven years before sale — a prospect that scares away the younger generation of mead producers.

The Presidium was created to promote and develop authentic Polish Mead to guarantee that the product is sold at a fair price on the market. Only then will producers overcome their fear of the initial investment and revive this ancient product.

**Production Area**
Poland
Around Warsaw

**Producers**
One family of artisans

**Presidium Coordinator**
Jacek Szklarek
Slow Food Convivium Leader
Tel. + 48 509 093034
jacek.szklarek@tosca.com.pl

# Polish
# Red Cow

**Saved by
Our Fathers**

The Polish Red Cow is a native breed that exists only in one small twelfth-century Polish Monastery with the unpronounceable name of Szczyrzycu. This breed has survived to this day thanks to the Cistercian monks of the monastery, who have maintained 80 breeding head there, about 100 kilometers south of Krakow.

Selected by one of Poland's most prestigious agricultural research centers, the Academy of Agriculture of Krakow, the remaining Polish Red Cows spend the months of May to October free at pasture and stay indoors the remainder of the year in efficient, modern stables, built by the monks with the help of the Academy.

Founded in 1234, the Szczyrzycu Monastery was once celebrated for its work in developing local agriculture. Until 1996, the monastery was home to a brewery, a small business that was returned to the fathers after the fall of Communism but proved too inefficient and economically infeasible due to its outdated machinery.

Today, the monastery owns 246 hectares of land that includes forests, pasture, and farmland. The friars want to recreate all the monastery's old industries: a bakery, a sausage factory, a jam-making workshop, beehives, and a brewery. But there is still a lot of work to be done and resources are few and far between. The first step in the project is to consolidate the herd of cows. A group of farmers in the region will receive a few head of Red Polish Cows and will rear them according to guidelines established by the monastery, which will in turn purchase all the milk produced.

## The Presidium

With the Presidium, Slow Food will attempt to help the monks establish a controlled production chain for both Red Polish Cow milk and, eventually, the cheese made from it. The principle challenge will be identifying the type of cheese suitable for production for the Polish market. In this region, no traditional cheeses exist apart from an unmemorable fresh acid-curd cheese.

Given that the Polish Red Cow produces excellent milk but no more than 10-15 liters of it a day, the production of quality cheese would be the only way for this breed to have a viable future. The Presidium will thus work to create a production protocol outlining how animals should be raised, to involve local farmers, and to develop a small cheese factory inside the monastery. Beppino Occelli, noted Piedmontese cheese ager and artisan cheese producer, will work with this Presidium to give technical assistance as well as supporting the project through the Slow Food Foundation for Biodiversity.

Photos ©optimaphotos.com

| Production Area | Producers | Presidium Coordinator | Presidium supported by |
|---|---|---|---|
| Poland | One herd is kept by the monks of the Szczyrzycu Monastery | Jacek Szklarek | Beppino Occelli |
| Krakow | | Slow Food Convivium Leader | |
| Szczyrzycu | | Tel. +48 509 093034 | |
| | | jacek.szklarek@tosca.com.pl | |
| | | | |
| | | Slawomir Wrzosinski | |
| | | Tel. +48 601287556 | |

# Mirandesa Sausage

### Mirandesa Beef and Bísaro Pork

In Portugal, inland travel and transport are made difficult by roads that wind around endless serre or hills—it can take up to three or four hours to travel a hundred kilometers. One can easily imagine what this distance meant for travelers 30 or 40 years ago, and the isolation and remoteness of Portugal's interior explains the survival of numerous tradition local products and native breeds.

Among Portuguese cow breeds, the Mirandesa is considered one of the most valuable and dates back to the Middle Ages. Most Mirandesa are raised on pasture that is occasionally enriched with hay, corn, oats and fava beans. There are over 800 breeders who raise Mirandesa totalling 4,700 head.

Like the Mirandesa language, the second language spoken in Portugal, the cow is an important source of identity in and around Miranda do Duoro in the extreme northeast of the country. The medium-sized Mirandesa is characterized by the tuft of hair on its forehead, its dark coat, and large, wide horns. The best cuts of Mirandesa meat are used for *assados*, or grills, while less-desired parts and the meat of older animals are added to lean beef and pork fat from Bísaro pigs to make smoked sausage. Raised semi-wild, this heritage breed of pig is identifiable by its black spots and large dangling ears.

To make Mirandesa sausage, beef is chopped by hand and combined with hunks of bacon, with the percentage of beef can vary from half up to 70% according to preference. The meat mixture is soaked in wine or in water with salt, garlic, bay leaves, and ground sweet and spicy peppers. After two to three days, the meat is removed, placed in pig intestine, and tied with a string. The sausage, or *chouriço*, is then cooked over a wood fire, left to dry, and smoked for three to four days. Once it is completely dry, it can be eaten either raw, grilled or boiled.

## The Presidium

The Presidium was created to raise the profile of Mirandesa sausage. The sausage, prepared during winter in the ranchers' homes, is made to exploit humbler cuts of meat or meat from older animals. Today, there are only a few producers who have the experience and manual ability to make this traditional product.

Thanks to a Portuguese law protecting regional cuisine, the three Presidia producers are allowed to make and sell the product, although it does not satisfy all hygeine laws. If promoted more widely, the sale of this *chouriço* would not be limited to local consumers. Both Slow Food and the Association of Mirandesa cattle breeders recognize that without a specific use for the less-valued parts of the animal, the work of a hundred breeders could be at risk. Those who raise the Mirandesa are passionate about keeping this hardy breed alive. Every year, the close-knit community of proud ranchers meets to celebrate the breed, with stands, bullfights, and an auction of the best animals.

**Production Area**
Portugal
Trás-os-Montes Region
Mirando do Douro

**Producers**
Three breeders and sausage-makers

**Presidium Coordinator**
Fernando Sousa
Associação de Criadores de Bovinos
de Raça Mirandesa
Posto Zootécnico de Malhadas
Tel. +351 273 438120-438121
mirandesa@ip.pt

**Presidium supported by**
La Montecchia

# Euskal Txerria Pig

**Black Basque Pork** Until the early 1900s, a small number of pigs could be found in every household in Spain's Basque territories. The pigs were taken to fairs to be sold to traders throughout Spain as *lichens*, or weaned piglets, when they were between two and three months old. One or two pigs were always kept to be fattened with table and garden scraps. In Basque country, as in the rest of Celtic Europe, the sale of live animals was a thriving business. At the time, there were three heritage pig breeds: the Batzanesa, the Chato Vitoriano, (both now extinct), and the Euskal Txerria. Thanks to actions taken by Pierre Oteitza, a French Basque rancher, the Euskal Txerria was barely saved from extinction. In 1997, only a small number of sows remained and there were no herds left in Spain's Basque territories. The Basque Government decided to support Pello Urdapilleta, a rancher, and Mariano Gomez, a veterinarian, the only people left working with local pig breeds.

Euskal Txerria pigs are characterized by their short legs, long floppy ears and black spots on their heads and rears. The Presidia pigs are raised naturally on acorns, chestnuts, hazelnuts and grass. Their diet is regulated only during the two months leading up to slaughter, when corn, fava beans and bran are introduced. Fattening continues until they reach a weight of 120 kilos.

Pello Urdapilleta, currently the only Presidium producer, cures the meat to make *chorizo*, aged seven months, which is 70% lean and seasoned with sweet paprika, salt, and garlic. He also makes *lomo*, aged five months, and *salchichón*, eaten fresh, and is now experimenting with *prosciutto*—ham cured Italian-style.

## Black Again

After fifty years of supporting a market dominated by conventional pig breeds, European farmers have rediscovered the continent's ancient breeds: rustic, free-range, and almost always with black pelts. Once commonplace, these black pigs—sometimes tinged with red, black-belted, or marked with white—began to decline in popularity in the mid-1800s, when Nordic pig breeds were first introduced to Europe. These new breeds, which were almost entirely without bristles and had white or pink skin, were developed to live in closed environments far from the sun, and were bred to put on weight quickly. In the twentieth century, interest in the growing Northern European pork market for lean, pink pork meat also greatly influenced the black pigs' numbers. The main centers of selection, Great Britain, Belgium, and Holland, sought to respond to these trends by selecting lean pigs. The portly black pigs, with their fatty, dense red flesh, are more suited for making cured hams or sausage and consequently fell out of favor. In Europe today, farmers are working to bring back the historic breeds—though many breeds are now extinct. The Spanish pioneered this movement at the end of the 1950s, working protect the local *cerdo iberico*, and the Portuguese followed suit, granting their Nero Alentejano a PDO for its cured Barrancos ham. Now, other European countries are running to catch up. French breeders have recognized five breeds and are developing new PDOs. In Italy, a range of new breeds are on the roster: the Black Nebrodi Pig, the Mora Romagnola, and the Casertana.

## The Presidium

This project was created to bring attention to the cured meats made from Euskal Txerria pigs and to motivate ranchers and local butchers to adhere to the methods put forth by Pello Urdapilleta. Guidelines will be established regarding raising and production in order to guarantee the traceability of the product.

For now, the cured meats are sold exclusively in Urdapilleta's restaurant and at local fairs. The Presidia hopes that the meats will be available in other restaurants and stores in Basque regions and that it will eventually be possible to sell them abroad.

In addition, the producers will be encouraged to meet with Spanish and Italian pork-butchers in order to improve the quality of the meats and particularly the hams.

| Production Area | Producer | Presidium Coordinator |
|---|---|---|
| Spain<br>Basque Territories | One breeder | German Arrién<br>Tel. +34 943322110<br>garrien@euskalnet.net |

# Gamonedo

### The Unknown Cheese of the Asturias

Just a few miles from the Cantabrian Sea, the verdant and dramatic Picos d'Europa Natural Park has deep valleys, high flat plains, and imposing jutting stone bluffs. The park is at the heart of Asturias, one of the most diverse regions of Spain, where the busy coast hems in a remote region whose economy is still based primarily on cheesemaking. This region is famous for Cabrales, one of the spiciest blue cheeses in Europe, as well as Queso de Treviso, Queso de los Beyos, and Gamonedo, a cheese made from the mixed milks of goats, cows, and sheep that is little known outside of Asturias.

A few small shepherds make Gamonedo high in the rugged peaks of Picos from May to October, though the cheese is also produced in the nearby valleys. In the mountain dairies, the cheesemakers work in small stone huts called *cabanas* and rear their animals in the land surrounding their dwellings.

To make the cheese, the milk is heated gently to 29-30°C and calf rennet is added. After an hour, the curds are cut to knuckle size and pressed. After a good deal of whey has flowed out of the cut curd, it is cut again by hand. Finally, the curds are pressed into

a mold and salted. The finishing of this cheese involves a light smoking: the cheese is placed on wooden board next to the hearth and dried for a few days by the warmth of the oak embers. Gamonedo is then aged in stone-lined caves for a minimum of two months.

After two months, the cheese has a milky flavor and crumbles in the mouth, leaving behind a lightly musky and buttery flavor. But after four to five months, the cheese fully blossoms, becoming creamy with a slight peppery flavor.

Gamonedo's pale yellow crust has bluish veins that usually extend all the way into the center of the white and crumbly cheese. This mold grows spontaneously, unlike the blue molds in cheeses like French Roquefort or Italian Gorgonzola, in which dried and powdered *Penicillium roqueforti* is added to the curd.

In Asturias, Gamonedo is served with cool cider, the traditional beverage of the region. Here, a glass is poured with élan, the server spouting it from the barrel over a meter away to oxygenate it before drinking. Like many blue cheese, Gamonedo also pairs well with sweet fortified wines.

### The Presidium

Presidium Gamonedo is produced from raw milk, weighs a minimum of two kilograms, and is lightly smoked. The best Gamonedo is matured four or five months and is best if kept in a cave during aging. A lot of work must still be done: the production protocol outlining animal feed needs to be defined, and above all, steps must be taken to protect the rare mountain shepherds who produce the most traditional version of this cheese. Every year, the number of small shepherds that persevere in this production diminishes, and with them the millennial civilization of the region will disappear.

The Presidium will work to restructure some of the remote aging caves and make them available to shepherds and valley cheesemakers alike.

To reach these objectives, the Piedmontese restaurant, hotel, and winery Castello di Verduno has adopted the Gamonedo Presidium, and the cheese is now a regular feature on the restaurant's menu. Gamonedo is a natural pairing for the Castello di Verduno's Verduno Pelaverga wine, made from a rare native vine that the Castello's winery has worked to protect and promote.

| Production Area | Presidium Coordinator | Presidium supported by |
|---|---|---|
| Spain | German Arrien | Castello di Verduno |
| Eastern Asturias | Slow Food Convivium Leader | |
| Municipalities of Cangas de Onís | Tel. +34 943322110 | |
| and Onís | garrien@euskalnet.net | |

Matching blue cheese and wine is an exercise that tasters find both exciting and frustrating. Wine and cheese with complementary flavors can be paired or they can be matched for contrast; a wine might be chosen to mitigate one excessive taste in the cheese with an opposite flavor. These pairings—however skillful—almost never completely avoid the basic incompatibility of milk and alcohol.

Mold-marbled or 'blue' cheeses are easier to match than some. Their sharp notes emerge from the stimulus of several alkaloids, which can be counterpointed with a sweet wine that acts as an emollient for the cheese's aggressive flavor.

Raisin wines—pressed from sun-dried grapes—have a high residual sugar content, and therefore pair wonderfully with piquant blue cheeses. For example, a Gamonedo

# Blue Cheese, Red Wine

with its light moldy veins and medium sharpness pairs well with a Tuscan Vin Santo, a Loazzolo, or a Beerenauslese.

A mature Stilton requires the accompaniment of a vintage Port, a well-aged Marsala or an Ice Wine. A naturally aged Cabrales has an aggressive sharp, astringent flavor, and therefore responds best to a rich sugary contrast: a Tokay Essetnia, a Recioto della Valpolicella or a Lagrima from Jerez. With Roquefort or an excellent cow's milk French blue, a Sauterne is a revelation.

# Jiloca
## Saffron

### Edible Gold

Saffron is one of the most expensive and least known spices in the world. Few people know where saffron comes from and how it is harvested, even though information about saffron is readily available.

Saffron comes from the stigma of a small crocus flower, the *Crocus sativus*, which is very adaptable and easy to cultivate, and originated in the eastern Mediterranean, a region that includes Macedonia, the Peloponnese, and parts of Asia Minor. Because of its versatility—it is used in religious rites and in tinctures, perfumes, medicine, cosmetics, and many foods—it has become part of the gastronomic and cultural traditions of many countries, including Spain.

Brought to the Iberian Peninsula more than 1,000 years ago by North African Arabs, saffron became an indispensable component in various traditional dishes. Like many spices imported to Europe in the age of discovery, saffron became a spice for the rich. It was so commonly used as a scent that the clothes and bodies of wealthy Spaniards and French once literally stank of saffron. Since those heady days, the production of saffron has changed greatly. Now, half-way through October, the saffron fields become colored a deep violet purple cut with dark red, which comes from the flower's precious stigma. When the stigmas are ready to be harvested, two or three weeks of heavy work begins.

First the flowers are picked, and then they are all laid out on a flat work surface. This is followed by the *desbriznado*, the most important phase of the operation, when the three stigma of the plant are separated from the blossom. To do this, the farmers hold the flower in one hand and delicately detach the three stigma from the blossom with index finger and thumb, working slowly to ensure that the flower does not break.

Jiloca has always been known for its saffron, locally known as *oro de los pobres*, or 'poor man's gold.' This area has the ideal climactic conditions for saffron cultivation; it varies from 700 to 900 meters in altitude and has long cold winters and brief, hot summers. In the past, Jiloca farmers always reserved a part of their land for saffron cultivation. When saffron was once still an important part of the local economy, everyone participated in the harvest and its taxing rituals of harvest and saffron thread cleaning with the help of hundreds of *azafraneras*, who arrived from bordering areas to assist in this labor-intensive work. The intense days of work concluded with a dance in the town plaza to celebrate the harvest.

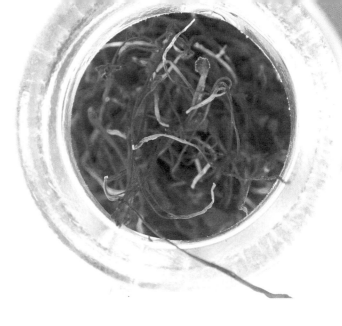

## Andalusian Recipes

Arabs first introduced saffron to Spanish cuisine, although the spice was known by the Romans and was imported in great quantities by them from their colonies. North African Arabs first codified many recipes that use saffron and are in part responsible for its popularity in Spanish cuisine.

The Spanish recipes that call for saffron are part of Andalusian cuisine, a regional cuisine that has many Arab elements. For example, the *arroz de Huerta*, a type of paella based on chicken, rabbit, green beans, hot pepper, and saffron that is made in the area surrounding Teruel. Even the simple *tortilla a la espanola*, with potatoes and onions, is enriched with a touch of saffron. Another favorite are filets of salt cod fried with potatoes and garlic and then baked in a thick and flavorful fish broth seasoned with saffron. But in the area where this spice is produced, there are many new ways to prepare it, like potatoes stuffed with onions, eggs, and saffron, or fried milk, a type of *crema catalana* also enriched with a touch of golden saffron.

## The Presidium

Currently, saffron produced in Spain is among the best in the world, since Medieval times, this spice has been at risk of being replaced by low-quality imitations. This project is being developed in collaboration with the *Museo del Azafrán* (run by the *Casa de la Cultura de Monreal del Campo*). Above all, the possibility of promoting Jiloca saffron among Spanish consumers is very promising. The price today for this saffron seems too high to many consumers, but given that a 100,000 flowers goes into making a kilogram of saffron, the cost is justified.

The Presidium will work to connect the communication about this product with guided tastings and comparative samplings of various types of saffron, including those made from lesser spices and addesd aromas. Organizing tastings of saffron are by far the most efficient means of explaining why this spice is so precious, as few other foods can convey such sensual pleasure.

---

**Production Area**
Spain
Teruel Province
Jiloca

**Producers**
Eight producers, only one of which sells directly under their own name

**Presidium Coordinator**
Chusa Portalatín
Tel. +34 976301408
chusap@terra.es

Spain

# Tolosa Black Beans

162

## A Taste of Oria

The shiny black skin of the Tolosa bean is a marked by a single white dot. When cooked in salted water with a drop of extra virgin olive oil, the beans become a dense and aromatic dish. Simply boiled, they become a delicious and velvety soup. This dry bean is unusual as it does not require soaking before cooking.

Tolosa beans were already being used and consumed at the beginning of the ninth century, and they have been cultivated in the Oria River valley for at least a millennium. The town of Tolosa is the center of production and every Saturday morning the town holds a covered market where local producers sell dry beans and, when in season, fresh Tolosa Black Beans. Each November, Tolosa holds a two-

## The Presidium

Eight years ago, producers from the Tolosa region began to save the best varieties of their black beans. Their project started modestly: every Thursday evening, a group would get together and cook, taste, and discuss the various bean varieties.

Eventually, they were able to select the two best varieties: one larger, called Handia, and one smaller, called Txikia. The tasting sessions led to the creation of an association of about fifty small producers.

The Presidium works to help the producers of Tolosa beans defend the integrity of their product. The Presidium will educate consumers and restaurateurs to allow them to distinguish real Tolosa beans from the inferior varieties sold under the same name throughout Spain. It will also support the traditional local market (pictured at left).

day festival to celebrate the new harvest.

Tolosa Black Beans are cultivated on small plots, with an average size of about an acre to a maximum of four acres. This crop grows best from 140 to 700 meters above sea level, and is often grown alongside crops like *guindilla*, a small green pepper. The farmers also grow corn and apples for cider production and occasionally keep cattle as well.

Tolosa Black Beans are planted from April to May and sprout in July. Once they begin to grow, the plants need to be tethered for support: traditionally, the beans are planted alongside corn stalks that act as a natural support; alternatively they are tied to a wooden frame of three sticks bound together at the top, forming a kind of hut; or the plants may also be tied to a special net.

Weeding is done by hand and trowel, and the plants are fertilized only with cow manure. The harvest takes place in October and is entirely manual. Once picked, the fresh pods are laid out on frames to dry. The beans are then husked either mechanically or, especially in the case of the smaller producers, by hand. Once husked, the beans are graded, sacked and stored.

**Production Area**
Spain
Basque Territories
Oria River Valley

**Producers**
50 farmers united in the *Tolosako Babarruna Elkartea*

**Presidium Coordinators**
German Arrién
Slow Food Convivium Leader
Tel. +34 943322110
garrien@euskalnet.net

Arantxa Ariztimuño
*Tolosako Babarruna Elkartea*
Tel. +34 943 650253
tolosakbabarruna@telefonica.net

# Reindeer
# **Suovas**

## Beasts of Burden in the Arctic Circle

Reindeer meat is the traditional food of the Sámi people, a native European tribe that live in an area called Sápmi, an arc of land spreading across the north of Sweden, Norway, Finland, and Russia. The Sámi speak dialects of an indigenous language of the same name and their culture has been shaped by the extreme cold and isolation of Sápmi. Here, winter lasts 200 days a year, during which temperatures sometimes dip below −30°C. During two fleeting months of summer, berries can be collected along with wild grasses and lichens, but the traditional food supply remains almost entirely dependent on the giant herds of reindeer that migrate annually to the mountains. Today, about 3,000 of the 20,000 Swedish Sámi are reindeer herders, a vocation that is limited to ethnic Sámi by law. The Sámi's reindeer are semi-wild and they pass the winter grazing in forests, moving to higher altitudes to graze in spring and summer. The Sámi are no longer nomadic—and some novelties such as helicopters and snowmobiles have radically changed the way they herd—but reindeer herders must follow their herds between the forests and the high mountains every season.

Much of the traditional Sámi food was developed to remain edible for the long periods when the nomadic Sámi were on the move. One of the most traditional preparations of this special, flavorful meat is Suovas. Suovas is prepared by dry-salting meat and smoking it in a traditional peaked hut for eight hours over an open fire. Suovas can be cut into pieces and grilled or eaten raw. Flavorful yet delicate, Suovas can be eaten in fine slices accompanied by pickled mushrooms and lingonberries. For long trips, the Sámi traditionally pack Suovas with unleavened bread to eat on the trail.

## The Presidium

This, Sweden's first Presidium, promotes Suovas made only from the tender meat cut from the reindeer's inner loin (*Innanlår* in Swedish) and brings together Suovas producers in Swedish Sápmi. Presidium Suovas is made from the meat of semi-wild animals that are slaughtered every autumn and winter; it is prepared throughout the year with the most traditional techniques of preparation, salting, smoking, and curing. The reindeer used to produce Presidium Suovas are not given any antibiotics or man-made feeds and graze entirely on the natural forage found in Sápmi. The Presidium is working to raise awareness of this ancient cured meat and to encourage the use of reindeer meat instead of introducing high-input domesticated animals that tax this Arctic region's delicate ecosystem.

## On the Back of the Reindeer

Reindeer figure prominently in the folk tales of the Sámi, reflecting the deep bond between this people and their semi-wild beasts of burden. Traditional stories tell of offerings to the gods made by piling up reindeer antlers and of angry gods that punish by killing a man's reindeer with a bolt of lightning. In the legends of the Sámi, the underworld is simply described as a snowy landscape populated by white reindeer. From the reindeer, the Sámi once produced everything they needed for their livelihood: reindeer skins were used to cover the tent poles of their houses; reindeer were milked, and their milk curdled with herbs; and intestines were stuffed with meat and fat and smoked. Today, just a fraction of Sámi are dependent on the reindeer. But the days when the reindeer was life and livelihood are in living memory, since many Sámi were nomadic up until 80 years ago. Now, in Sápmi, there are ethnic restaurants, big chain supermarkets, and all the trappings of modern Europe. But the reindeer remains a central aspect of Sámi life, irregardless of how the context has changed. As Olov Sikku, a reindeer herder, says, "I love to try new things, but I still eat like a Sámi. For example, I love Italian pasta, but the only sauce I can stand to eat it with is roasted reindeer bone marrow."

| Production Area | Producers | Presidium Coordinator | Presidium supported by |
|---|---|---|---|
| Sweden<br>Swedish Sápmi | Eight herders and artisans | Ola Buckard<br>Tel. +46 70 328 44 55<br>ola.buckard@chello.se | Sámiid Riikasearvi<br>(The Association for the Protection of Sámi Culture) |

# Muggio Valley Zincarlin

## Peppered Cheese from the Swiss-Italian Border

Zincarlin is produced in the mountains on both sides of the Italian-Swiss border near Lake Como. On the Italian side the cheese remains little more than a faded memory of *zincarlino* or *cingherlino*, a fresh goat's milk cheese made by shepherds in the Generoso Mountains in the province of Varese.

Just over the border in Switzerland, a cheese with this strange name is still made in the Muggio Valley. Zincarlin is a raw milk cheese seasoned with black pepper; it is usually made from cow's milk, but sometimes, small quantities of goat's milk are also added. Its shape resembles an upturned cup and it weighs about half a kilogram. One of its distinctive features is that the curds are never broken but just left to drain for a day and a night straining in a cloth. Some cheesemakers assist in draining out the whey by making a cross-shaped cut in the curd. After draining is complete, the mass is energetically kneaded with pepper and salt and then molded into shape by hand. Zincarlin can be eaten fresh but benefits from being aged for two or three months, which gives it a more developed taste and aroma. Maturing is carried out in cool

## The Presidium

Well-aged Zincarlin scarcely exists any more as the Muggio Valley cheesemakers sell almost exclusively fresh cheese. The aim of the Presidium is to recover the traditional version of the cheese, aged for at least one and a half months and produced using raw milk. It is complex work, with the various stages requiring a demanding effort by the producers involved. It is necessary to identify the appropriate production methods and obtain a stable product, find suitable premises for aging, carry out tests to determine the right proportions of the mixed milks and conduct sensory analysis to develop the most viable and traditional version of the aged cheese.

semi-underground cellars; the forms are sometimes placed inside terracotta jars called *ole*, which help to keep the cheese moist and soft. For the same reason some producers treat the crust with white wine or grappa. Zincarlin is transformed during its aging process: the crust becomes reddish-gray, the cheese becomes soft and fatty, and its taste and aroma are enriched in their complexity and persistence.

| Production Area | Producers | Presidium Coordinator |
| --- | --- | --- |
| Switzerland<br>Muggio Valley | Three cheesemakers | Luca Cavadini<br>Slow Food Convivium Leader<br>Tel. +41 91 6841816<br>slowfoodti@bluewin.ch |

Photo Alain Le Garsmeur, Corbis/Contrasto

# Artisan Somerset
# Cheddar

## Cheddar as You Never Knew It

Cheddar is one of the most famous cheeses in the world but also one of the cheeses most often produced industrially. Barely 5% of the 400 producers who made Cheddar in the cheese's home territory—the county of Somerset in southwest England—a half-century ago remain in business. The centralization of cheesemaking in the years following World War II had significant effects on traditional Cheddar production in Britain. First, official requirements for cheese to have specific moisture content (to enhance keeping properties) led to the elimination of moister types. Secondly, the number of farms that resumed production after the war was greatly reduced. The introduction of rindless block cheeses and frequent use of pasteurized milk further reduced the unique characteristics of Cheddar made in southwest England. But an artisan, handmade version still exists, made in the rich dairy pastures surrounding the town of Cheddar in Somerset, where a few farmers continue to produce the region's traditional cheese.

The cheese curd is created using old strains of bacteria (known as 'pint starters'; these are based on traditional local microflora) and calf rennet, both of which help to provide broad, round flavors. The curds are cut until they're about the size of a grain of rice, then they are poured onto a draining table where the real work begins. The curds are 'cheddared' by being formed into blocks, which are stacked and turned by hand for an hour. This changes the texture from crumbly lumps to pliable, elastic slabs and gives the finished cheese its unique texture. Before being transferred to the aging room, the slabs are bandaged with lard-soaked muslin. During the aging process, the cheese's natural crust remains intact and is never shrink-wrapped or treated in any way to aid moisture retention. A single form of Presidium Cheddar weighs 50 to 60 pounds, and is aged for at least 11 months, though it can be aged up to two years.

Artisan Somerset Cheddar has a richly moldy brownish gray rind and an intensely hay-yellow curd. The texture is firm yet buttery, and the curd has flavors of caramelized milk, hazelnut, and bitter herbs.

## The Presidium

All three Presidium members make only ten to twenty cheeses a day and—from start to finish—each form takes three days to make. Presidium members only use milk produced on their farms and they use it, untreated, within a day of milking and solely local 'pint starters' are used to culture the milk. The Presidium has been created with the goal of educating consumers about a different type of Cheddar made from fresh local raw milk and crafted by hand. This Presidium will also promote taste education, participate in local and international gourmet events (where the presence of an 'artisan' Cheddar often raises eyebrows), spread the understanding of traditional British farming techniques, and adopt sustainable cheesemaking and agricultural techniques.

**Production Area**
United Kingdom
Somerset County

**Producers**
Three cheesemakers

**Presidiium Coordinator**
Randolph Hodgson
Tel. +44 20 7645 3550
randolph@nealsyarddairy.co.uk

# Cornish Salt Pilchard

## A Mediterranean Classic from Cornwall

A fish with a tapering silvery body covered in shiny scales, *Sardina pilchardus* sardines are known as pilchards when they are caught mature off the coast of Cornwall in southwestern England. These sardines swim to England from the southern Mediterranean, and when they arrive in Cornwall they are fatter and longer, reaching 35 cm.

During the pilchard season, which lasts from June until March, small fishing boats sail out for a few hours at sunset to cast their traditional seine nets. The length of the net, the depth to which it is lowered and the size of the mesh are carefully considered so that only pilchards are caught. Once the nets have been drawn up and the boats are back in port, the fishermen take their catch to be salted.

After curing—whole, not gutted—for a few weeks in sea salt, the fish are taken from the large curing vats and packed into wooden boxes where they are gently pressed to extract excess water and oil. They are then packed in wood-staved barrels, where they can mature for up to a year. Cornish Salt Pilchards taste similar to salted sardines, although they are meatier and the use of the whole ungutted fish gives them a lightly bitter tang. In Italy, still their primary market, they were traditionally the most economical salted fish available and figure heavily in peasant cuisine in some coastal regions such as Liguria. They are used as a base for rustic pasta sauces along the coast near Genoa and also grilled after soaking in milk and water to remove excess salt. At the beginning of the twentieth century there were dozens of plants salting pilchards in Cornwall to supply the booming Italian, French, and Spanish markets. Across southern Europe, Cornish Salt Pilchards were sold from traveling carts in the remote mountain regions. The market slowly dried up and, by the 1960s, only one plant continued to pack Salt Pilchards in Cornwall.

## Protestant Pilchard Packer's Papal Prayer

At the end of their season, protestant Cornish pilchard packers toasted their Catholic customers with the following saying:

Here's a health to the Pope, and may he repent,
And lengthen by six months the term of his Lent.

It's always declared betwixt the two poles,
There's nothing like pilchards for saving of souls.

Seventeenth-century Cornish toast, from *Cornish Seines and Seiners, A History of the Pilchard Fishing Industry* by Cyril Noall. (D. Bradford Barton, Truro, 1972).

## The Presidium

Today, one plant, The Pilchard Works, continues the ancient tradition of salting pilchards using methods and equipment that date back almost a century. It has been designated a 'working museum' by the British government, and is thus allowed to continue using its antique equipment to produce barrels of salt pilchards for shipment to Genoa and further afield.

The Cornish Salt Pilchard Presidium was created to recognize one of the British Isles' most historic foods, which dates back to the 1500s, yet is almost nonexistent today. The Presidium is made up of the last remaining pilchard salter along the Cornwall coast and the four fishermen who work closely with him. The Cornwall pilchard fishery is a model small-scale fishery, and the methods of the fishermen involved in the Presidium are recognized as sustainable. The Presidium will work to revive the dwindling Salt Pilchard market in southern Europe and to help develop a new market for the Salt Pilchard in Great Britain.

| Production Area | Producers | Presidium Coordinator |
|---|---|---|
| United Kingdom Cornish Coast | One pilchard packer and four fishermen | Nick Howell Tel. +44 1736 332112 nick@pilchardworks.co.uk |

# Gloucester
## Cheese

## Single and Double

The county of Gloucestershire, which comprises both the Cotswolds and the low-lying Severn Valley, has been a center of British cheese production for centuries. The making of cheese for export from this region has been documented as early as the eighth century, though no records exist describing the nature of early Gloucester cheese. Signs of the region's cheesemaking history dot the landscape: traditional farmhouses in the region are often equipped with a special third-story cheese-aging room with louvered windows and many of the region's festivals and celebrations include cheese rolling. As early as 1500, the city of Gloucester was famed for its cheese, butter, and meat markets, and two centuries later the region's Double Gloucester cheese was regularly exported to the North American colonies.

The original Gloucester cheese was a colored cheese made from full-cream milk from the local Old Gloucester cow. Today, Gloucester cheese has two versions: Double and Single Gloucester, which are linked by history and a common ancestor, but that have evolved in the past two centuries into quite different products.

The cheeses were so named because the Double is a richer full cream product, while the Single was frequently made of part-skimmed milk or when the cows were on inferior forage. The Double Gloucester was designed for durability, was made from full-fat milk and was sold nationally. The Single was the cheese that the poorer, local people ate, made in thinner forms from partially skimmed milk after the butterfat had been taken off for butter.

Traditionally, Gloucester cheese was produced with milk from the local Old Gloucester cattle breed, which produced milk with small fat globules and high protein content exceptionally well suited to cheesemaking. Sadly, as the production of Gloucester cheeses boomed, the use of traditional Old Gloucester cow's milk was phased out. The animals could not compete with the specialist dairy breeds for gross milk production, and were gradually replaced by Longhorns, Shorthorns and, finally, the black and white Holstein Friesians. By 1975 only one viable herd of Old Gloucesters remained, yet today through the concerted efforts of the Gloucester Cattle Society, the breed is no longer quite so endangered with close to 400 breeding females now surviving.

## Can Milk and Beef Coexist?

Once upon a time, most cows served three purposes: they produced milk, were slaughtered for beef, and worked on the farm.

In the past two centuries, bovine breeds have been selected for one type of production to the point that their efficiency in one field excludes it in other areas. Some breeds were super-developed for milk production (like Fresians) while others were selected for meat production. The third role these cows had on the farm—as beasts of labor—was more or less eliminated by the changes caused by the mechanization of agriculture.

In rare local breeds, however, these two characteristics still exist in the same animal. Combined with free-range grazing, these breeds naturally produce both incredible meat and flavorful, highly-scented milk. This milk, clearly, is produced in low quantities compared to the yield of high-output Fresian cows.

Old Gloucester cows are one of these cross-specialty breeds, as are many of the Presidia for rare breeds. In Italy, one exemplary of this dual-purpose adaptability is the Podolica cow, a hardy and resistant breed that is officially classified as a meat breed but that produces such excellent milk that it is considered responsible for the quality of some of Southern Italy's greatest *caciocavallo* cheeses.

Evidence suggests that, although these dual-purpose breeds do not produce much meat or milk, what little they do yield is well worth it.

## The Presidium

The Presidium was created with the cooperation of the Gloucester Cattle Society to recognize the long established link between the Old Gloucester cow and Single and Double Gloucester cheesemaking. The Presidium will encourage farmers in Gloucestershire and bordering counties to take up and maintain the ancient art of traditional raw milk Single and Double Gloucester cheesemaking to the highest standards using milk from Old Gloucester cows. It will work to develop local distribution for the resulting cheese and to encourage retail outlets to source these local products.

| Production Area | Producers | Presidium Coordinator |
|---|---|---|
| United Kingdom<br>Gloucestershire County | Two cheesemakers | Charles Martell<br>Tel. +44 01531 890 637<br>charlesmartell@lineone.net |

# Old Gloucester Beef

## A Dual-Purpose Breed

The Old Gloucester is one of Britain's oldest native cattle breeds and was once common throughout the West Country. Once referred to simply as the Gloucester cow—for its eponymous home county—the name 'Old' has been added in recent years. Old does not refer to the breed's antiquity, but is a local slang term, which means 'dear' or 'affectionate'—a sign of the deep esteem locals had for this breed. The Old Gloucester was already well known in the thirteenth century, when it was used for beef, milk, and draft work on Gloucestershire farms. The Old Gloucester's fortunes began to decline in the eighteenth century with the development of more specialized meat and milk breeds. Interest revived around 1896 when the last two herds were divided up and sold to various breeders, but the numbers continued to dwindle as newer breeds gained in popularity. By 1930 only 142 Old Gloucesters remained, and the Gloucester Cattle Society stopped operating. In 1972, when only one viable herd remained, the Old Gloucester breed was classified as endangered. When the breed reached this critical point, close to extinction, local farmers cooperated by reforming the breed society to save it, and in the past thirty years they have brought it back from the verge of disappearance.

The Old Gloucester has lived in Gloucestershire for nearly a millennium and is a remarkably hardy and well-adapted animal for the region. It thrives with little care and produces fine quality meat that improves with the animal's age, reaching its peak when a cow is over two years old. The beef is currently experiencing a renaissance with local food lovers, who find it well adapted for the traditional local dishes that involve slow cooking. It is exceptionally flavorful and pairs well with Gloucestershire's traditional Tewkesbury mustard seasoned with horseradish.

## The Presidium

The Old Gloucester Presidium was created with the Gloucester Cattle Society to raise awareness of the eating quality of the beef of this traditional breed. The Presidium includes all breeders of pedigree Old Gloucester beef, who finish it for a minimum of six months in the county of Gloucestershire (though it may be raised in neighbouring counties or further afield). The Presidium will work to develop local distribution for Old Gloucester beef and to encourage chefs to source this locally raised, rare breed beef.

Given that the Old Gloucester is still a breed at risk, the Gloucester Cattle Society encourages breeders across the United Kingdom, though the long-term goal of the Presidium is to revive the breed fully in its home territory, to which it is exceptionally well-adapted.

**Production Area**
United Kingdom
Gloucestershire County

**Producers**
99 breeders united in the Gloucester Cattle Society

**Presidium Coordinator**
Charles Martell
Tel. +44 01531890637
charlesmartell@lineone.net

# Three Counties Perry

### From Ancient Trees

Perry is a little-known traditional English drink made from the fermented juice of perry pears—small, bitter fruits with such a high level of astringent tannins that they are almost impossible to eat raw. Perry has been made in Southern England for centuries, and the name 'perry' once referred to all wild pear trees as well as to the beverage. The trees bear viable fruit only after a few decades of growth and the best can be over a century old. The ancient perry orchard is a classic part of the British landscape and its tall, majestic trees provide the basis for an important ecosystem, considered a unique habitat by British naturalists. There are over 100 different varieties of perry pears, but many varieties only have a few remaining specimens and are in danger of disappearing completely. Perry, like cider, was once made on the farm for the farmer's family and workers and is not suited to large-scale production, as the production of each batch varies greatly with the mixture of pear varieties used.

The method for producing perry is the same as that of producing hard cider. The fruit is harvested, milled to a pulp, and pressed to extract the juice, which is then fermented: some perry undergoes a second in-bottle fermentation to make a sparkling beverage. Almost all British perry is produced in the 'three-counties' area of Herefordshire, Worcestershire and Gloucestershire, and is consumed almost exclusively in the region of production. It is a classic accompaniment to traditional British cheeses such as Single and Double Gloucester, Cheshire, and Lancashire. Real perry contains no additives. It can be dry, medium or sweet in taste, and still or sparkling. The quality can vary from 'rough' like scrumpy hard cider to an almost wine-like drink. The flavor of farm-made perries is variable: they may be fermented to dryness but will retain a distinct pear aroma.

## Orchard Ecosystems

The classic English orchard has widely-spaced, thick-trunked trees with low-hanging branches suspended over a tame grass lawn; it does not, at first sight, look like what could be called a 'natural' environment. Cows or sheep trim the grass, the trees are clipped back regularly, and everything looks improbably in order. But in England, which has a history of intensive use of agricultural land, and where it is virtually impossible to find a patch of earth that has been left in a 'wild' state, these orchards have become an ecosystem in their own right, as important to the English countryside as forests, bogs or wetlands. Long-established traditional orchards may have a long history of continuity on the same site. Although most of the trees in the orchard will be upwards of 100 years old, the orchards itself may have existed upwards of 800 years on the same patch of land. The surviving traditional perry pear orchards often contain old-fashioned varieties with evocative names such as Clipper Dick, Bloody Bastard, Lightning Pear, Merrylegs, Startle Cock, and Stinking Bishop (often a single pear variety will be limited to just one orchard). The advocates for the preservation of old perry tree orchards have often been more environmental advocates than promoters of traditional gastronomy, though the conservation of the traditional habitat is as important for the taste quality of traditional perrys and ciders. The orchard's biodiversity is important on a microscopic level as well. The best yeast strains often come from the orchard itself, and perry may be pressed outside among the trees to facilitate traditional yeast growth.

## The Presidium

Under present market conditions the remaining perry producers are struggling: few of them make a living from producing only perry, and many of them produce it in their spare time simply because of their love of their product and its heritage. There is little or no marketing of perry and the tiny local market continues to diminish year after year. There is now increased awareness amongst the producers of the need for high quality standards if perry us to be promoted among attentive consumers. The Three Counties Perry Presidium is working to raise awareness of high-quality perry made from the bitter perry pears—not from fleshy cooking or eating pears. The Presidium is also working to establish guidelines for a select group of producers to stabilize quality, while retaining the natural variety of a product made from various perry pear varieties. The Presidium producers are working to define the full list of the pear varieties traditionally used for perry production.

---

**Production Area**
United Kingdom
Counties of Herefordshire,
Worcestershire and Gloucestershire

**Producers**
Ten artisans

**Presidium Coordinator**
John Fleming
Slow Food Convivium Leader
Tel +44 1584 875548
info@slowfoodludlow.org.uk

# Index by Product Type

## Cheeses

Aged Artisan Gouda - *The Netherlands, 140*
American Raw Milk Cheese - *United States, 84*
Artisan Salted Butter - *Denmark, 112*
Artisan Somerset Cheddar - *United Kingdom*, 168
Gamonedo - *Spain*,156
Gloucester Cheese - *United Kingdom, 172*
Irish Raw Cow Milk Cheese - *Ireland*, 136
Niotiko - *Greece*, 128
Oscypek - *Poland*, 146
Texel Sheep Cheese - *The Netherlands*, 144
Tibetan Plateau Yak Cheese - *China*, 94
Zincarlin - *Switzerland*, 166

## Fruits and Nuts

Andean Fruit - *Peru*, 80
Pando Brazil Nut - *Bolivia*, 38
Pozegaca Plum Slatko - *Bosnia-Herzegovina*, 108
Purén White Strawberries - *Chile*, 66
Umbu - *Brazil*, 52

## Legumes, Tubers and Vegetables

Andean Potatoes - *Peru*, 82
Canapu Cowpea - *Brazil*, 42
Juçara Palm Heart - *Brazil*, 46
Pardailhan Black Turnip - *France*, 116
Quebrada de Humahuaca Andean Potatoes - *Argentina*, 34
Saint-Flour Planèze Golden Lentil - *France*, 122
Tolosa Black Beans - *Spain*, 162
Yacón - *Argentina*, 36

## Cereals, Minor Cereals and Rice

Andasibe Red Rice - *Madagascar*, 18
Andean Corn - *Argentina*, 32
Anishinaabeg Manoomin - *United States, 86*
Bario Rice - *Malaysia*, 102
Criollo Corn - *Mexico*, 76
Dehradun Basmati Rice - *India*, 98
Red Fife Wheat - *Canada*, 54
Tehuacán Amaranth - *Mexico*, 78

## Animal Breeds

Blue Egg Chicken - *Chile*, 56
Euskal Txerria Pig - *Spain*, 154
Gascony Black Pig - *France*, 114
Giant Istrian Ox - *Croatia*, 110
Heritage Turkey Breeds - *United States, 90*
Old Gloucester Beef - *United Kingdom*, 174
Potosì Llama - *Bolivia*, 40
Polish Red Cow - *Poland*, 150
Rennes Coucou Chicken - *France, 118*

## Oils

Argan Oil - *Morocco*, 22
Mustard Seed Oil - *India*, 100

## Crustaceans, Fish and Mollusks

Calbuco Black-Bordered Oyster - *Chile*, 60
Cape May Salt Oyster - *United States, 88*
Cornish Salt Pilchard - *United Kingdom*, 170
Eastern Scheldt Lobster - *The Netherlands*, 142
Irish Wild Smoked Salmon - *Ireland*, 138
Robinson Crusoe Island Seafood - *Chile*, 68

## Cured Meat

Mangalica Sausage - *Hungary*, 132
Mirandesa Sausage - *Portugal*, 152
Reindeer Suovas - *Sweden*, 164

## Cacao, Coffee and Spices

Chinantla Vanilla - *Mexico*, 74
Huehuetenango Coffee - *Guatemala*, 72
Jiloca Saffron - *Spain*, 160
Mananara Vanilla - *Madagascar*, 20
Merken - *Chile*, 64
Monkó Cacao - *São Tomé and Príncipe*, 26
Nacional Cacao - *Ecuador*, 70
Sateré Mawé Native Guaranà - *Brazil*, 48

## Wines and Fermented Beverages

Mavrotragano - *Greece*, 124
Polish Mead - *Poland*, 148
Roussillon Dry Rancios Wine - *France*, 120
Three Counties Perry - *United Kingdom, 176*